WHO SPEAKS FOR GOD?

GERALD KENNEDY

WHO SPEAKS
FOR GOD?

ABINGDON PRESS
New York • Nashville

WHO SPEAKS FOR GOD?

Copyright MCMLIV by Pierce & Washabaugh

Library of Congress Catalog Card Number: 54-9196

Scripture quotations unless otherwise designated are from
the Revised Standard Version of the Bible and are copyright 1946, 1952 by the Division of Christian Education of
the National Council of the Churches of Christ in the U.S.A.

SET UP, PRINTED, AND BOUND BY THE
PARTHENON PRESS, AT NASHVILLE,
TENNESSEE, UNITED STATES OF AMERICA

THIS IS FOR

M Y M O T H E R

who believed on Him
and never died

PREFACE

WHETHER THESE CHAPTERS SHOULD BE REGARDED as sermons, essays, or lectures, I really do not know. They have been preached, written, and lectured. A sermon loses its essential nature when it has to be read, and a lecture is often a longer and duller sermon. The only thing I want to say is that these ideas seemed to me worthy of emphasizing and drawing to the attention of my contemporaries.

The general theme hit me after thinking about Norman Cousin's recent title *Who Speaks for Man?* That implies responsibility enough, heaven knows, but what about the man who speaks for God? The book is an attempt to consider that high calling and some of its implications.

This material first took shape in a series of sermons I preached last summer at the First Methodist Church of Pasadena, California. Then it was presented as the Mendenhall Lectures to the ministers of Indiana at DePauw University in Greencastle, Indiana, in February, 1954. My thanks go to President Russell J. Humbert and the faculty and students of DePauw University for their hospitality.

GERALD KENNEDY

May, 1954
Los Angeles, California

8

CONTENTS

9

I

Who Speaks for Persons!

And to love one's neighbor as oneself, is much more than all whole burnt offerings and sacrifices.
—MARK 12:33

You shall not oppress a stranger; you know the heart of a stranger, for you were strangers in the land of Egypt. —EXOD. 23:9

NORMAN COUSINS WROTE A VERY PROVOCATIVE AND significant book entitled *Who Speaks for Man?* which is always an important question to ask, especially in a day like ours. In the midst of the divisions, nationalities, orthodoxies, and ideologies where is the voice speaking for all mankind? The world needs philosophers who see beyond the limited horizon of a particular class or station and become a voice for men in their essential, universal nature. We have had too little of that, and the brilliant editor of the *Saturday Review* is on the right track when he seeks a voice for humanity. The religious man, however, is aware of an even more important and essential question, though it has not been so considered in

11

recent decades. Much more significant than the voice of man is the voice of God, and the real question is: Who speaks for God?

The Bible includes two mighty affirmations which have to be comprehended if it is to be read with understanding. It assumes for one thing that God does speak to men because he is the God of the living and not of the dead. God confronts individuals and societies with his demands and his promises, and it was the genius of the Hebrew people to be sensitive enough to hear his voice in a special way. The more they listened, the more convinced they became that their God was one who speaks. The second great affirmation of the Bible is that men may and must speak for God. There were times when his divine demand made their words run contrary to the popular opinion about them. There were times when to speak for him put their own lives in jeopardy. But when the prophet said, "Thus saith the Lord," he had an authority which made him unwavering and sure. The Christian faith finds itself speaking for man when it is at its best, but it speaks for man only because it speaks for God.

It is this faith and assurance which we seem to have lost in modern times. Henry Steele Commager of Columbia University put it in these words: "It may be doubted whether at any time in three hundred years religion had meant so little to Western man as it meant in the first half of the twentieth century.'' The clamor has been for the right of men to speak their minds, and they have had little hesitancy in declaring not only what is good for themselves, but for their neighbors. Yet the voice of God has seemed strangely silent, and the man who announces that he speaks for God is looked upon as a fanatic or as one enamored with an archaic figure of speech. We are in need of discovering those principles which have guided the men who claim to speak for God, for we are desperately in need of hearing his voice this day.

When we turn to Jesus, we hear him tell a young lawyer that the center of the whole law is to love God and to love one's neighbor as one's self. Jesus begins with the assumption that if a man is to speak for the Father, he must speak for persons; and this is a good place for us to begin. You may say that one sure sign of the divine validity of the Word of God is that it is always for men and it is always to persons. We may be sure, therefore, that when a man claims he is speaking for the Eternal but does not have this personal element in his message, his credentials are forged. He who speaks for the God of Israel and for the One revealed by our Lord

13

Jesus Christ will speak always for the sons and daughters of the Father.

1. Not Systems

One of my friends, a colleague in the Council of Bishops, told me about an experience which illustrates the kind of thinking many of us are doing today. He was attending a banquet and sat next to a professor in a state agricultural college who began telling him about some of the work the faculty was doing throughout the state. One man was an expert on hogs, and he spent part of his time visiting with farmers and telling them how to improve their breed and increase their income. Another man was an expert on poultry disease, and he went around telling farmers how to keep their flocks healthy. Still another was a cattle expert, and he advised cattlemen in regard to methods which would increase beef production. At this point my friend remarked that there were some counties in the state without a doctor. He thought it would be a wonderful thing if the state university could provide medical experts to visit these counties and advise families regarding the health of their children and encourage the prevention of sickness. At once the professor looked at him with

14

critical eyes and asked abruptly, "What are you, Bishop—a socialist?"

Now the thing that strikes me as remarkable about this question is its attempt to escape from the issue. It was entirely beside the point so far as my friend's suggestion was concerned. He was thinking only of persons and of human need, but the professor had fallen into the habit of thinking in terms of systems and general categories. The question for the professor was no longer one of a particular service to a particular person, but only a matter of discovering whether or not the question seemed to fit an orthodox system of thought. That this is a general contemporary tendency is apparent to any man who talks to very many people. Too many Americans would rather ignore the human problem, or pretend that it does not exist, than answer it in a manner that does not fit the pattern of their accepted political or economic theories. It is a sad day when a man's mind no longer apprehends persons but sees only systems. Nothing could indicate more clearly our contemporary misunderstanding of the kingdom of God than the attempt of many sincere but limited Christians to equate the kingdom with their favorite form of society.

The substitute of systems for persons always

leads to an unrealistic approach to life. Because we are dealing with something secondary rather than primary, we transform means into ends. This leads us away from the straight path to truth and takes us wandering through all kinds of underbrush and over the edges of ravines. It substitutes cliches and a jargon for the realistic analysis of the problems. Our conversation becomes full of high-blown phrases which nobody understands precisely, but which give a comfortable feeling of treading on good, safe ground. If we stop and think of such talk for a little while, it becomes apparent that most of these phrases can be brought down with a common pin.

Remember Hans Christian Andersen's story "The Emperor's New Clothes"? They were supposed to be of a marvelous filmy quality never seen before. The emperor walked before his people and received their enthusiastic acclaim. Then a child ruined the whole thing by blurting out, "But he has got nothing on." Thus does a mind uncaptured by an ideology probe to the truth.

Systems are rigid, and their formulations tend to get out of date. They may have had living meaning at the time they were first formulated, but as time goes on, they become descriptions of good, old days which no nostalgia can bring back to us again. They tend to set up straw men and

16

knock them over instead of facing the real enemies. It is only a living spirit that can be the
same yesterday, today, and forever, and never
a system.

I heard a labor leader say that in the early
days of the labor movement there was a spon-
taneity that kept it close to the real life of work-
ingmen. On one occasion a rather pompous expert was making a speech when a man from the
back of the hall interrupted with an appeal to
the chair. The chairman ignored him for as long
as possible, but finally he had to stop the speech
and ask the brother what he wanted to say.
Everyone was astonished but secretly pleased
when this untutored brother said simply, "Mr.
Chairman, my point of order is that Brother
Blank has been speaking for fifteen minutes and
he ain't saying nothing." The man who has given
his allegiance to the system which does not
change and grow speaks much and says little. I
always have a strange feeling that such a man is
speaking like a voice from the dead about matters which have become so academic that they no
longer are relevant.

But not only does the spokesman for a system
become unrealistic; he also becomes untruthful.
The Christian defines truth in terms of life,
which is to say that it is revealed in persons and

17

particularly in the Person who was the revelation of God. Follow a system consistently and it will lead you off on a tangent. Life is not completely logical but is always full of paradox and seeming inconsistency. When the law becomes our criterion, and not life, we do not end up with truth.

It is necessary at all times for men to ask concerning a political system: What after all is its chief purpose? The danger of a period that finds Capitalism and Communism at each other's throats for a final decision is that we shall begin to think that any man's definition of capitalism is something to bow before without questioning whether or not it may have missed the way. I happen to believe that capitalism, as we have shaped it in America, is much to be preferred over communism or any other system yet devised. But I believe it because I think that persons can best be served through a capitalistic system. If we forget that any social organization is to be judged by the way it can serve persons, we shall be tempted to make an idol out of it and fall into the sin of idolatry. That is what happens when men perform crimes against individual dignities and freedoms in the name of the political system which is supposed to guarantee those liberties. The man who speaks for

18

God must be aware that man is a political animal and that political systems are important, but he must be aware also that the importance of the political system lies in its ability to serve persons. Changing conditions demand changing methods, and to hold to outgrown methods because of a loyalty to an irrelevancy destroys our integrity and encourages the lie.

One of the great secrets of our country's progress has been her refusal to become doctrinaire economically. We have been properly suspicious of orthodoxy in any realm. We have been singularly blessed in a leadership which has kept our eyes on the job to be done and our attention directed toward the welfare of all the people. Thus we have believed in free enterprise but have not hesitated to regulate that free enterprise whenever it was necessary for the common good. We send our mail by a government-owned postal service, but we send our telegrams through a private corporation. I lived in a city one time where part of the citizens bought their electricity from a private company and others bought it from a publicly owned utility. We are educated by means of the public schools, and we are healed by doctors whose official association makes it clear that they are opposed to being socialized.

This is the strength of the nation and not its

weakness. An attempt to substitute some iron-bound system for the freedom of experimentation and variety is not the American way. When we compare the results of our mixed economic order with any nation that has tried to be consistently one thing or the other, we must be impressed by the superiority of our approach. When a job needs to be done, it will happen sometimes that one method is better than another. To use the method best adapted for the particular job will keep our economic thinking where it ought to be—namely, face to face with the needs of persons rather than bowing before a particular system.

Similarly a theology which comes to be an end in itself proves to be utterly unchristian in its understanding of man. The Calvinism which carried its thought to an ultimate conclusion was regarded by John Wesley as having confused God with the devil. The theologian who wants to regard God as "wholly other" soon ends up in an impossible cul-de-sac, where he has simply to ignore the heart of Jesus' revelation of God. In an attempt to achieve theological consistency we end up with a strait jacket around our thinking, which is appropriate only for the unbalanced and more at home in a padded cell than in the society of free men. At the center of realistic

Christian theology there is always the assurance of God's concern for man, which found its best manifestation in Jesus Christ. Once this concern has been relegated to the background, our thought may lead us to some kind of logical consistency; but it will never lead us to the truth.

So much religious controversy through the years would have been impossible if we had stayed closely to the Gospels and dwelt less in the academic controversies of the Fathers and the medieval theologians. A great mind like Paul's can never go far wrong, because he is primarily not a theologian spinning fine theories, but a missionary dealing with the problems of his mission. When we go back to Jesus himself, we are even more impressed with realism and truth because he simply would not teach systems nor be confined to rules. His thought, from beginning to end, reflected his faith that the Sabbath was made for man and not man for the Sabbath. No institution, however good it might be in itself, was to be thought of as worthy of man's final allegiance. He spoke for God, and his whole life and teaching were directed toward persons.

In one of the best homiletical books I ever read, Nathaniel J. Burton's *In Pulpit and Parish,* there is a reference to Sir William Hamilton's lectures on metaphysics. In discussing the

21

human memory and telling what it has been able to do, Sir William referred to a young Italian who could listen to 36,000 words read and then repeat them in the same order. He could even turn the list around and repeat it backward. He could recite the list skipping every other word and do all of this after a year or two had passed. Then Burton concludes with these words: "I do not now remember what else he could do—and do not want to remember—the thing is frightful enough already. But did you ever hear of that man among the really great men of history?" [1] And I quite agree with the noted preacher. The Italian had a wonderful gift no doubt, and such a memory is almost beyond our belief. But true greatness does not lie in the field of developing a perfect system of memory or of anything else. It lies, finally, in the service a man renders to people and the extent to which his life is dedicated to persons. No matter what a man's reputation or credentials may be, they are not from God unless he is a spokesman to men as men, for persons as ends in themselves.

2. Not Humanity

One thing that seems clear from the history of reform movements is that when the focus on in-

[1] New York: The Macmillan Co., 1925. P. 285.

dividuals gets blurred and reformers begin to think of men in bulk, they nearly always go wrong. In the name of some future utopia and claiming a deep concern for unborn generations, the most horrible crimes can be committed against individual men just now. There is a line in Homer in which the gods decide "to destroy men so that there may be a song for future generations." Nietzsche was angered by that line, and he wrote: "Thus we suffer and perish so that poets should not be short of subject matter —and this is decreed by Homer's gods, who seem to care very much about the amusements of the coming generations, but very little about us, who are alive now." Those who cannot see the value of a man but can comprehend only the value of men are never to be trusted, even when they are sincere. The crimes committed in the name of service to humanity by monsters who started out as well-meaning reformers are legion.

The rebellion of the French peasants against the intolerable conditions which the nobility had fastened upon them is one of the inspiring chapters of human history. It is good to know that there is a line beyond which the tyrant cannot pass without unleashing in the people a consuming anger which will destroy him. In that great upsurge of common men in their search for justice we see the divine nature of humanity asserting itself. We can agree that in that time it must have been bliss to be alive, and to be young was very heaven.

But how quickly the disillusionment set in, and how soon the great hopes died! Within what a short period the great words of liberty, equality, and fraternity became tarnished. For the revolution fell into the hands of men who began to substitute humanity as the object of their service rather than persons. Then they could perform the most horrible crimes in the name of liberty and turn the revolution into a new dictatorship. It is one of the ironies of history that the movement which began as the liberation of common men bequeathed to the world the system of universal military service. It was a people's revolution which forced every man, whether he would or not, to become cannon fodder that Napoleon's lust for conquest might be satisfied. He who speaks for God does not speak for an amorphous lump called humanity.

In more recent times we have watched the Nazis make obedience the ultimate virtue in order to build a reich that would last a thousand years and bring status and glory to the German people of tomorrow. The testimony of those who knew him best and were themselves betrayed by

24

him indicates that Hitler paid attention to individuals only so long as they were valuable to his larger plans and only until they were no longer able to assert any independence. It is no wonder that his religion was the old Norse paganism rather than Christianity, for he was wise enough to understand that the Christian insistence on the significance of each man was the last thing in the world which would serve his cause. He needed the gods who were tribal gods and national gods, but the God who seeks the lost was an embarrassment to him and a judgment on everything he hoped to accomplish. As long as you are serving the humanity of the future, you can find justification for getting rid of all troublesome individuals in the present.

But even more recently and more dangerously we are face to face with another tyranny which liquidates by the thousands to safeguard the classless society of tomorrow. In some ways it is even more blunt and honest than previous regimes, because it announces frankly that the individual is not significant but only that vague, impersonal thing called the *state* really matters. Yet in Communism's early pronouncements there was held out a hope which a good many Western liberals accepted as valid. There were so many Communist pronouncements in the early

25

days that sounded like echoes of the New Testament teachings. The idea that the strong should bear the burdens of the weak, or that each man should produce according to his ability to serve those in need, sounded benevolent and loving.

It has become the fashion in our time to smear every man who at one period in his life believed that this approach held out hope, even though he may have dropped the whole thing with horror when he saw what the Communist tyranny really meant. But let us understand that the fatal flaw in it was not easy to observe at that time. Communism's evil consists simply in making future humanity the object of its worship while denying that separate souls have inviolable dignities. An atheism which denies God is inevitably bound to deny his children soon or late, for the setting-up of humanity as the final value is to lose sight of that which gives a man his meaning. What all systems have in common, if they hold humanity as the object of their devotion, is an inescapable temptation to manipulate men for purposes which may sound very good and justifiable. But the manipulation of men is a confession that you have put something above men. You have confessed thereby that they have become objects and not persons, and they are to be used for the convenience of their betters.

There is a significant passage in Rilke's *The Notebook of Malte Laurids Brigge*. The young Brigge is speaking of poetry, and he says:

> To write a single line one must have seen many cities, men and things. . . . One must have had the memory of the groans of child-birth, and of the pale and sleeping forms of those who have given birth, their bodies now disburdened. One must also have been with the dying, have watched by the dead with the window open to the sound of the world's stir outside. And it is not enough to have memories.[2]

These words could be written not only of poets but of men who would speak for God.

It has seemed to some political reformers especially that Jesus was lacking at the point of having more specific schemes worked out for the betterment of men. Political scientists, economists, and sociologists have wondered why he did not become more precise in tracing out the plans for the Christian society. He seems to have been unnecessarily vague in this field, keeping his teaching in the realm of the personal and directing his commandments toward individuals. But there is no surer sign that he spoke for God than that he spoke constantly to persons. He never let himself become lost in humanity, and

[2] Tr. John Linton (London: Hogarth Press, 1930).

he never substituted some future reform for present kindness. So Christians through the years have agreed with John that when they saw Jesus, they were seeing God.

One of the discoveries of our modern society is that we do not get very far when we deal with men in the bulk. Industry has learned this. One of the great advances made in American industrial relations is management's recognition that labor is not just a commodity to be regarded and treated as any inanimate product. It is this part of our industrial story which we have failed to tell clearly enough and powerfully enough to peoples of the Orient who are suspicious of what a capitalistic society has to offer individuals.

I have been impressed with the growth of an enlightened recognition that men must have pride in themselves and in the part they play in production. There was a local physician in England who discovered just before Christmas that a number of his patients had not paid their bills for over a year. He wrote each one a kind note canceling the bill and expressing his sympathy that they had had such a poor year. All but one of them paid immediately. So big business has come to see more and more that it takes something besides pressure, sanitary working conditions, or even recreation facilities to create

28

the kind of relationship which means prosperity for all. The word has to reach man's sense of individual significance and responsibility. It is hardly too much to say that the great advance made in this field has been the discovery that you have to begin to think of laborers rather than labor.

The Church must never forget this truth, and in our time it has been tempted to forget it. When a church gets too big, it turns into a kind of religious factory which deals with humanity in the bulk rather than with persons. Our worship of size in the Church has not proved to be wise. The work of the Kingdom is done where the Christian fellowship exists and where personal relationships bind the members to one another and to God. The Church can never speak for its Lord if it speaks for social reform in general but has no precise word for the man with a broken heart or for the woman with a broken dream.

The greatness of the missionary enterprise has been its ability to create small fellowships which have become demonstrations of God's concern for people. Take away the missionary enterprise around the world, and the great reservoir of good will for our country which we are so rapidly dissipating would never have been filled up in the first place. The Church at its best has always been a voice straight to the heart of each man, bringing him out of the lostness of the crowd into a direct and personal relationship with God.

I am troubled in these days by so much talk in church circles about mass communication and mass evangelism. I am as anxious as the next man to find the way to get to the people with our message. I do not agree, however, that the Church can ever do its work via television or any other mass media. Let us use these things to the limit of our ability. Let us understand at the end of the day that it is in the Christian fellowship that men step out of their anonymity as simply units of the crowd and come face to face with God.

A woman in a church I served one time had more real concern for the big causes than any individual I have ever known. She would spend any time necessary to organize a group or to serve on a committee, if it had a world-wide program. She would take the time to write letters to her Congressman expressing her opinion about pending legislation. But her home was always a mess, and the children never looked quite clean or very well tended. The meals were haphazard affairs, which provided nourishment but no aes-

thetic pleasure. Her husband always impressed
me as a man who suffered from low spirits.
Sometimes it seemed to me that in her desire to
serve something far away she was overlooking
her most important calling right in her own
home. I was reminded of something Georges
Duhamel says in his *Journal de Salavin*. He remarked that certain saints of an Indian religion
swept the ground before them whenever they
took a walk so that they would not crush any in-
sect. But he wondered why they failed to understand that as they used their brooms, they must
have been breaking the feet of the little creatures
which they were pushing out of the way. It is
so easy to envision the faraway and overlook the
immediate.

In the early days it was the custom at Yale
University to have a sermon preached at the
commencement. One year the General Association of Connecticut chose the Rev. George Per-
kins to preach the sermon. But knowing that he
was a man prone to discuss slavery on every
occasion, they took the precaution of giving him
a subject; and it was "Christian Sanctification."
They went into the church on the Green that day
confident that this time the powerful antislavery
speaker would have to confine himself to another
subject, which they had no doubt he could do

31

because he was "considerably sanctified himself." But the congregation was taken aback when they heard the preacher's first sentence come forth: "The greatest hindrance to sanctification in this country is slavery." [3] How hard it is for some men to come down to the congregation's immediate plight, but how easy it was for Jesus. This is not to say that we shall not deal with the great, broad subjects, for there is nothing affecting man which is foreign to our gospel. But it is important that we should begin at all times with a word to a person and not to a crowd, and speak to the man before us rather than to the absent and faraway.

3. The Common Man

There is a great text in the Old Testament which does much to shed light on the democracy Israel gave to mankind. The words were written into the law of the people: "You shall not oppress a stranger; you know the heart of a stranger, for you were strangers in the land of Egypt" (Exod. 23:9). It was a command that Israel should not forget the lonely and the isolated, for they themselves had been foreigners and slaves. Being a stranger is part of every man's fate, and when the people dealt with one who

[3] Burton, *op. cit.*, p. 346.

came from the outside, they were to remember the days when they were outsiders in the land of Egypt.

It is the insight of our faith that we are to speak for the common man, which does not mean that we are to speak for the poor, as such, or the uneducated. We are to speak for that which is common to all men and never assume that special treatment is to be reserved for certain groups and denied to others. The man who speaks for God has always a universal note, as he speaks for persons who in spite of differences are one in their heritage and destiny.

It would be foolish to deny that there are real differences among men. Any man who travels out beyond the confines of his own city soon learns that other communities do things differently. We know, for example, that the British drive on the "wrong" side of the street, which is to say they drive on a different side of the street. But we do not even need to go abroad to discover the different habits people fall into within the same nation. They have different customs, and they have different accents.

Whenever we are in the midst of a struggle, we tend to exaggerate the differences between us and our enemy. During the Second World War, for example, an English nobleman wrote a book to prove that the Germans were from the beginning quite outside the pale of civilization. He made a rather imposing case by carefully selecting certain data. There were a large number of people quite ready to accept a thesis that proved the Germans would have to be exterminated. But this proposition could be maintained only by ignoring a vast amount of other data which denied it. Any man who has been to Germany and participated in the religious life of that country can never believe that the differences are as deep and lasting as Vansittart would have us believe.

During the war the Japanese were portrayed as being so different in their customs and attitudes that we never could find a common meeting ground. I heard intelligent men say seriously that Japanese soldiers were able to live on practically nothing, that they felt no pain, and that their scale of values were so different from ours that we might as well try to talk with men from Mars. But a visit to the Japanese Church brought me face to face with Christian people whose likenesses impressed me much more than their differences.

Let this be a warning to those who would speak for God in times of crisis. We need to hear the insistence that the Russians are people. While the common man of that unfortunate country is twisted around by an evil tyranny, we may yet discover the means of communication direct to him. Once we have shut our minds to the possibility of a meeting place or of a common nature, we make our plans blindly and our attitudes and policies become twisted and warped. The healing word so often is the testimony that even the enemy is a part of God's family, with deep desires not unlike our own. This is necessary if we are to be realistic in our dealing with the enemy and if we are to arrive finally at the solution of the problems which prevent peace.

We do not have to be appeasers or sentimentalists in order to hold before our generation the insistence that all men have fundamental virtues and vices which they hold in common. John Brown of Edinburgh in a biography of his father refers to his uncle Ebineezer, an old Scottish clergyman, who insisted on preaching as long as he could ride. He started out one day in a heavy snowstorm to fulfill an appointment, although every attempt was made to discourage him. But he went anyway and finally fell off into a drift, where he and the horse were wallowing helplessly when some rough fellows came along carting whiskey to the town. They lifted him up and put him on his horse, gave him something from their cart to warm him (he was not a Methodist) and made every attempt to help the old man. The next time the presbytery met, uncle Ebineezer rose to speak, which was unusual, for he hardly ever had anything to say at the meeting. "Moderator," he said, "I have something personal to myself to say. I have often said that real kindness belongs only to true Christians, but (and then he told the story of those men). More true kindness I never experienced than from those lads. They may have had the grace of God, I don't know; but I never mean again to be so positive in speaking of this matter."[4] For everyone who is sure that you can divide men into categories, it is a good thing to have the category smashed and to realize that in the most unexpected places you find kindness and in the least expected places you sometimes find vice. We had better learn to speak for the common man.

This is a good test to apply to a politician's speeches. After some experience as a legislator Senator Lodge from Massachusetts wrote in the Harvard classbook for 1949, "Life as a legislator has on the whole made an optimist out of me—about both the United States and human nature." Then he went on to say that "the interests which men have in common are more

[4] *Ibid.*, p. 117.

numerous and important than those which drive them apart" and that "the really evil politician is he who seeks to stress the things which divide." Apply that to some of the brethren who make the headlines of our time and see what it indicates. He who serves God will serve men by emphasizing their common nature and their common interests.

This is the great task of the Church. When a church loses its place as the meeting place of all classes and conditions of men, it has betrayed its Lord. An Oxford professor reports that a friend of his was taking part in a church river picnic and overheard a girl on the bank asking her companion who the people in the boats were. The other girl replied, "I can't imagine who they can be; they're all such different types." And as George B. Caird goes on to say, she had paid the church a very high compliment; for here was an association that transcended social barriers.[5]

If men are the sons of God, then they find their unity in him. It is interesting to note that Jesus was attacked most bitterly because he assumed that this was true. The practical men of society do not like to have any strong witness that their

[5] *The Truth of the Gospel* (New York: Oxford University Press, 1950), p. 107.

little barriers and their little defenses of status are false and stupid. Once we have lost our pride, we know that we stand side by side with every man as brother—whoever he is and whatever his position may be. The Pharisee and the publican have to pray together, because each is guilty of sin and stands in need of forgiveness.

One of the beloved and effective preachers of the days past was Father Taylor, a Methodist minister sometimes called the "sailors' preacher." Because of his deep concern for the poor and his feeling that the gospel was a word of salvation for such people, he had little patience with Ralph Waldo Emerson, whom he regarded as having paganism, pantheism, and uncertainty all mixed up together. But when he met Emerson, he was more confused than ever, because he said that Emerson's opinions must keep him out of heaven but his good character would certainly keep him out of hell, and there did not seem any place to put him. It is a good thing to leave such matters to God and in the meantime to know that when we speak for the common man, we speak for God.

4. The Neighbor

In a certain department store in Portland, Maine, there seemed to be a regular wave of shoplifting at one of the busiest counters. It was all stopped finally when the manager hung a huge mirror back of the counter, so that anyone in the customer area could see himself from any angle. There is a sense in which our neighbors are always mirrors of ourselves. When we are face to face with a family across the street, we are also face to face with ourselves; and we never get lost in generalities or vague hopes which are impractical. It is this mirror of the neighbor which Jesus holds before us constantly, to keep us honest, realistic, and sane.

The most astounding thing about our relationship with God is that he comes to us directly through the Incarnation. His language is personal, for the Incarnation is the language of God. With all the different manifestations of his presence and his will, he reserves the direct approach to us through a Man. It is like the King stepping down from his throne to share with his humblest subjects the long plans for the Kingdom and the important part which each citizen must play. The personal God who speaks through persons to other persons is the living God who has made personality the ultimate clue to all the mystery of his creation.

Humanity finds itself turning time and time again to the priest, and the priestly function of the ministry must not be minimized. We need someone to tell us about God's grace in such fashion that we who are not mystically minded may receive it. The help we need has to be brought very near, or it will be always out of reach. As a fine Christian teacher one time said, "It is strange that God should seem distant until a human voice brings Him near; that His promises once seemed idle until we saw a human face lighted by them; that a month's striving will sometimes bring us, not to faith but to despair, and then five words from stammering lips will break the frost and free our souls." [6] We are the ones who are commissioned to speak for persons because we speak to them in the name of the God whose relationship is always personal.

This is an immediate demand that we must not deny. It is an existential experience which confronts us daily with the human situation and its claim upon us. It is the man next door for whom we speak, and for the lost and confused persons who are seeking the Christian fellowship in the Church. Jesus never went very far, geographically speaking. His ministry was confined to a very small area, yet in that area he found the experiences and encountered the hopes

[6] William Russell Maltby, *Obiter Scripta* (London: Epworth Press, 1952), p. 62.

and fears which would not have been different if he had roamed over all the world. There in that little land with its slavery, its persecution, its poverty, its glorious history, and its dark destiny he spoke for God as no man ever spake before or since. By his own life as well as by his teaching he told about the reward which comes to one who gives a cup of cold water. He will not let us forget that in the day of judgment the question is always a man's relationship with his neighbor. There is a sense in which every great revival movement since his time has been a simple rediscovery that God's word is for every man's neighbor.

There is a famous colony of mercy in a place called Bethel near Bielefeld in Westphalia. It is dedicated to the care of epileptics and the mentally deficient. It is in some ways a horrible place to visit, and perhaps its most pitiful part is the ward for babies and young children. Some years ago a wealthy man was being shown about, in the hope that he would help to support this colony, which depends upon gifts from interested people. He was finally taken into the children's section, where he was so moved that he could not speak. After he had recovered himself, he asked how many of the children could be helped enough

41

so that they might live normal lives. "About one in a hundred," was the reply.

"Oh," the visitor said impatiently, "then it isn't worth it."

Then the superintendent replied quietly, "Suppose that one were your son?" [7]

In the midst of mass movements and general programs the one who speaks for God brings men face to face with each individual and asks, "Supposing this one poor child were your son?" For we have learned through the example of our Lord that ninety and nine can never take the place of the one who is lost and that in the economy of heaven every individual soul has eternal worth. He who speaks not for systems nor for humanity but for the common man and for the neighbor has been given the authority to speak for God.

[7] C. T. Leber, *World Faith in Action* (Indianapolis: Bobbs-Merrill Co., 1951), p. 305.

II

Who Speaks for the Spiritual!

> For the bread of God is that which comes down
> from heaven, and gives life to the world. They said
> to him, "Lord, give us this bread always."
> —JOHN 6:33-34

> Why do you spend your money for that which is not bread,
>   and your labor for that which does not satisfy?
> Hearken diligently to me, and eat what is good,
>   and delight yourselves in fatness.
> —ISA. 55:2

IN THE FOURTH GOSPEL, JESUS SEEKS TO BREAK
through the spiritual dullness of his contemporaries and help them see the underlying spiritual nature of men and of life. He does not succeed always, for even his disciples found it difficult to accept as real what was so obvious to him. Jesus shows us men who believed in what they could see and touch, but with little perception or appreciation of the unseen and undefinable. The great gap between Jesus and even his closest friends was his spiritual awareness, which they never fully comprehended or shared.

But the people of the first century were not

unique in this failure. Isaiah spoke to a generation who invested in the ephemeral and thought it was substantial. They spent money for bread that perished and for that which was not bread. The food for their souls was free and available, but they could not bring themselves to ask for it. Always religion has to make the attempt to help men believe in the spiritual realities, and always it is difficult and never more than partially successful. Most men can accept this truth generally, but they cannot accept it concretely. It may be true in eternity, we will affirm; but we cannot accept it as true for today. If I may use an overworked term in contemporary theology and philosophy, it is hard to accept the spiritual reality existentially.

To us who strive sincerely to speak for God today, there comes the conviction that the people have ears but hear not; eyes they have but see not. The extreme materialism of our life is demonstrated by the sentimental view we take of spiritual matters. Like poetry which we hear but do not understand, so the talk of unseen things sounds pious and pleasant. But we do not see how it has any practical meaning for us, and we do not really believe it anyway. We would be the first to resent any man denying the importance of the spiritual life, but we are also the last to insist that a man ought to live as if it were real.

It has become popular in our time to refer to religion in all kinds of speeches. It is not unusual for the service-club orator to pay lip service to the need of a return to faith. He may even get applause at that particular point in his address, but he never gets precise because he has not the foggiest idea what religion is and what its demands are; neither have most of his audience. It is a part of the same strategy which has learned the advisability of including a few patriotic sentiments in the remarks and speaking a good word for mother, home, and heaven. Our concept of spiritual religion is usually sentimental and emotional only.

Americans need to be brought face to face with the power of unseen influence. They need to realize that their lives are governed by ideas and ideals, that thoughts march and dreams have legs. It is a shock for practical-minded men to be confronted with the truth that attitudes, values, sentiments, hopes, beliefs, philosophy, rule the world and direct the future. That the real truth about a civilization is its religion and its spiritual assumptions is a scandal to the contemporary mind. But the measure of a man is his creed, which he does not need to recite because he reveals his actual spiritual assumptions every

45

day. The persuasive forces are not always logical propositions, but they are words which stir the imagination, songs which fill the heart, and thoughts which haunt the mind. We may assume that spiritual matters are secondary, but a careful scrutiny of our history proclaims that the real issues are of the mind and the spiritual decisions are the lasting, influential ones. An age of specialization needs a new appraisal of the decisive importance of the liberal arts in education.

It may be assumed by some that our country is an exception to this general rule. Surely, one might say, here we have been molded and shaped by science and by the physical conquest of a continent. Of course we have been affected by these mighty projects, but the lasting United States is an idea and a hope. It is founded on a faith which becomes more apparent when we have to face a relentless foe whose program is a denial of what we have believed.

Eric F. Goldman in a significant article entitled "Books That Changed America" began with these words: "Ever so often it happened America would be rushing along, staking out farms and throwing up factories, exulting and worrying and denouncing, and suddenly somebody, facing a stack of blank paper, would touch the paper with magic. A book appeared and things were never quite the same."[1] He developed the thesis that no important change ever took place in this country without a book preparing the minds of the citizens for it. He maintains that no matter what sudden shift the United States may seem to take, it will not be lasting unless there has been a shift in the thinking of the people. This I believe.

We come then to the necessity of penetrating into the minds of men, if we are to affect their lives. We will fail to make a lasting improvement unless the inner life has been touched. At the end of the day, physical changes are not so important as psychological changes. To put it in the words of my theme: If you would speak for God, you must speak for the spiritual.

> And man is a spirit
>   And symbols are his meat,
> So pull not down the steeple
>   In your monied street.
>
> For money chimes feebly,
>   Matter dare not sing—
> Man is a spirit,
>   Let the bells ring.[2]

[1] *The Saturday Review,* July 4, 1953, p. 7.

[2] "Holes in the Sky." Copyright 1948 by Louis MacNeice. Reprinted by permission of Random House, Inc.

47

1. The Mystery of Man's Nature

Sometimes a novel appears which has the power to make actual what has been vaguely felt. By bringing into sharp focus an important truth, it brings the reader into a new experience and creates for his life a new dimension. Such a book is Vercors' *You Shall Know Them.*[3]

It has an interesting and unusual plot, which is obviously a means of bringing certain problems and questions before a generation which has tried to ignore them. The plot is contrived, we may say; but it never gets in the way of the main purpose of the book. A strange tribe of jungle creatures are found which have some of the rudimentary characteristics of humanity but also seem to have obvious likenesses to the animal kingdom. The question is whether they are to be regarded as men or as beasts. The issue is important because if they are only animals, they can be hunted and exploited. But if they are men, then they have certain rights and status. Incidentally the more recent conclusions of anthropologists and students of evolution suggest that the novelist is not dealing with an impossible situation. There is a growing agreement that the "missing link" was a creature with a brain about

[3] Tr. Rita Barisse (Boston: Little, Brown & Co., 1953).

48

the size of an ape's, but he walked like a man and he had essentially a human body.[4]

A young scientist tests the matter when he puts to death the offspring of a man and a female of the tribe. He goes on trial for his life, and the question is whether he is a murderer or simply a man who has killed an animal. In the English trial which follows, evidence is brought from nearly every possible source; and testimony is offered from every point of view. Science, philosophy, anthropology, zoology, religion, all give their judgment as to the essential criterion of humanness. They discover that there is no general agreement, and while we blindly assume that the term "humanity" is definable, actually it is not, except within limited circles. Where is the line, and what is the basis for announcing that this creature is a man, but that other one is not?

While the mystery is never cleared up entirely in the novel, as indeed it never will be on this earth, the conclusion is finally established that somewhere in the realm of religion the answer must be found. In other words, to probe the heart of man's mystery, you must turn to man's spir-

---

[4] See Ruth Moore, "Evolution Up to Date," *Harper's Magazine*, Nov., 1953, pp. 84-89. Her book, *Man, Time, and Fossils* (New York: Alfred A. Knopf, Inc., 1953) tells the story in more detail.

itual nature. Paul's ancient categories of "natural" men and "spiritual" men were good ones, for they indicated then and they indicate now a significant dividing line. The clue is not in exterior characteristic, nor is it in any material fact. It lies somewhere in the deep places of man's soul. It has to do with his sense of wonder and his feeling for the sacred and the holy. It is rooted in his demand for worship and in his hunger for fellowship with the divine. We wish we knew how to be more exact, but it is a great thing to be able to proclaim with assurance that man's spiritual life is not an extracurricular activity which he plays with when he gets civilized, but the center of his being. Speak for the spiritual!

There is this matter of conscience, for instance. It is strange that with all our research and consideration we cannot achieve any simple, generally accepted definition of what it is. Nor can we find general agreement as to what conscience implies regarding the nature of man. The explanation is always framed in reference to a presupposition so that it does not come to us from an objective point of view. This is true of most things to a considerable extent, of course; but in the matter of conscience it is nearly always approached as a piece to be fitted into a puzzle.

50

Hardly ever does a man begin with the fact of conscience and follow the deductive path.

This much seems plain—conscience is a stumbling block to all those who would treat men as mere automatons. The behaviorist can never make a satisfactory place for it in his system, try as he will. There is always something strained and unreal in his explanation, and he has to contrive a definition of conscience that leaves out large and important parts of its function. What does it mean that a man has a sense of something owing to himself? How does one account for the fact that a man has a conviction of something owing to his neighbors? And greatest mystery of all, how can we come to terms with a creature who is unable to escape the conviction that he owes something to God?

Conscience makes it impossible for men to enjoy evil. We may quiet the inner voice in the rush and excitement of difficult endeavor, but after it is over, the voice will not be quiet. Our success, instead of bringing us our heart's desire, brings us tension, restlessness, and guilt. So Sholem Asch's *A Passage in the Night* relates the tale of a successful man who after retirement cannot escape the haunting memory of beginning his career by stealing a purse from a poor man. His family sends him to a psychiatrist,

who convinces everyone but the man himself
that this is all illusion springing out of the strict
religious training of his childhood. He is committed to a sanatorium, where he does not get
well but gets steadily worse. When at last a rabbi
convinces the family that there was a theft and
there can be no healing until the man is allowed
to make restitution, the broken life is restored. It
is amazing how we get too wise and too clever to
grasp the elementary fact that a man has a conscience and he has to live with it.

We must stop treating this part of our nature
as if it were a neurosis to be diagnosed and dis-
posed of through scientific exorcism. Joyce Cary
relates an unhappy time in a boy's childhood
when he lied and trembled with the sense of his
guilt. Then he says:

I do not remember anything but the terror—possible for
a very short time before I was found out, and punished,
and so absolved. The fear of hell, the punishment of sin,
how the modern parent revolts from such teaching. Yet I
will assert that far from doing us children harm, it was a
sure foundation to the world of our confidence, a master
girder in the palace of delight. For we saw its justice, we
knew, in the common phrase, exactly where we were—the
wicked would be punished, and the good should have reward.[5]

[5] *Except the Lord* (New York: Harper & Bros., 1953).

Men do not know where they are until they come to terms with conscience. This is a very ancient truth about us, proclaiming our spiritual nature; and nothing has happened to modify it or make its dismissal possible.

A thief broke into the home of a Presbyterian minister in Elizabeth, New Jersey. When the family returned, they found the house ransacked but nothing taken. The minister's sermon notes were scattered about on the study floor, and the only explanation seemed to be that the thief had read the notes and had a sudden change of heart. Thus does conscience attack us in the most unexpected places and under the most unusual circumstances. There is no defense against it.

Another fact of human nature is its demand for worship. It is true, as has been said so often, that men are incurably religious in that they will worship something. If they do not bow before the Lord their maker, then they bow before the gods of their own making. But something out beyond men haunts them with an insistence that they are only partially alive until they have been found by God. This is never a matter of choice but of necessity.

The experience is that One puts his demands upon us, as he has a perfect right to do. There is some truth in the idea that the man who staggers up the street drunk is on a mistaken quest for God. That is, there is truth in it if we do not assume that men are excused for their wrong choices and will not have to pay for them. Here we need straight thinking, which warns us that the cost of worshiping the idols is more than we can ever afford to pay. But humanity can never be understood until we realize that we are God-seekers not by choice but by nature. Nothing can go right with us until our worship is directed toward God, and there is no anthropology that is more than surface speculation if it does not begin with this foundation truth.

After the Titanic sinking in 1912 an American newspaper put two drawings side by side to describe the disaster. One of them showed the ship striking the iceberg and being smashed, and underneath were these words: "The Weakness of Man, the Supremacy of Nature." The other picture showed a man stepping back to give a woman and her child the last place in the last lifeboat. Below was the caption: "The Supremacy of Man, the Weakness of Nature." [6] That artist managed to sum up in two drawings an essential truth about the mystery of human nature. It does not lie in our knowledge nor in our spectacular

[6] Ralph W. Sockman, *How to Believe* (New York: Doubleday & Co., Inc., 1953), p. 33.

achievements in the physical world. It lies in the spiritual qualities of personality. He who would speak God's word to men will speak directly to their spirits. And not, mark you, because this is the nice thing to do, but because this is the center of man's uniqueness and the place where his decisions are made.

2. Society's Recognition of Man's Spiritual Nature

A large, shiny Cadillac approached an intersection where a traffic light had turned red. The driver moved deliberately into the lane reserved for pedestrians, so that people crossing the street had to go around the car. An old man started across the street, came to the car, looked at it with an air of displeasure, and paused to consider what ought to be done in such a circumstance. Then deliberately he opened the back door of the car, walked through leaving both doors open, and went on his way. I like that! He seemed to be saying that there are some things you cannot do even if you drive an expensive car. There are some rights which have to be preserved even if a man is on foot. He was announcing that every member of a society has a dignity which must not be violated.

This is something that a nation forgets to its own cost. When we look back of the American

Revolution, we have the feeling that our revolutionary ancestors made a mountain out of a molehill. At least when we consider that period and our own, George III seems like a relatively benevolent ruler compared with Hitler or Stalin. The issues of taxation and religious liberty do not impress us as critical. What was all the fuss about anyway?

For one thing, it was about the rights of citizens to be treated as ends and not means. These pre-Americans had the feeling that their economic life was controlled by men whose chief interest was in the welfare of the mother country and not in the welfare of the colonies. Decisions were made not in the light of what might be good for the colonists themselves, but always in the light of maximum prosperity for England. Our fathers would not stand for it, even if they had to run the risk of war. The winning of the war, which was a long chance, would condemn them to all the uncertainties of independence; but no matter, they would be their own men and make their own decisions. They were proclaiming that to be pushed about for the benefit of other men is intolerable even when the alternative far from guarantees comfort.

But the other objection of the colonists seems even more farfetched to us—namely, the issue of religious liberty. Why would men leave security for a wild, untamed new country just to worship according to their conscience? That seems the height of sentimental foolishness to the men of our time. But our fathers believed that nothing is more significant than a man's religion, and he cannot practice it bound by the regulations of a state institution. He must be free personally to worship God, for this is an affair having to do with his immortal soul. Let us not forget that our country's essential greatness lies not in its overwhelming material power but in the heritage of free men who stood before a world full of tyranny to announce that because men are spiritual creatures, their worship of God must be without hindrance or proscription.

In all the discussion of the conflict between Russia and the West, there is one element which is discussed very little; yet I believe it to be the crucial one. It is the difference between the Communist philosophy of man and the Christian doctrine of human nature. The Communistic system of Russia cannot endure any more than Napoleon's empire could last. Remember that Victor Hugo said Napoleon fell because he embarrassed God. And Communism with its atheism and its assumption that man is only of material importance as a member of the state will go down because it too is an embarrassment to God. It is sentimental and unreal in its estimate of humanity. Men will not long endure being treated as cattle, and the ultimate downfall of such a system is written by the Creator in the stars and in the heart of man.

It has been argued in recent times that India prospered more economically and politically under the rule of Britain than will be possible under an independent government. Whether that is true is debatable, but for the time being let us assume that it is true. It is argued that Asia would prosper more with colonial status under the control and guidance of the West than will be possible split up in a myriad of sovereignties. For the time being let us allow that also. But none of this argument goes to the real point, which is that men, because of what they are, must be free to have a voice in their own affairs. Profit is not the final issue here, but the nature of man. Political destiny is shaped by spiritual forces.

A government must never forget that its citizens are persons. The temptation is to think of them as taxpayers, or consumers, or draftees, or as population statistics. The disease of bureaucracy attacks government officials and swells their egos to the place that they are no longer servants but manipulators. In the name of that colossus the state they assume that the lives of individuals are to be subjugated to the rule of policy. When this disease runs far enough, it destroys a nation because it undermines the spiritual foundations upon which a society must rest. Power worship is not only evil in its implications but suicide for a people because it pushes them over the abyss into spiritual insanity.

One of the most difficult relationships to establish is that between a man and his country. Where does the individual conscience enter the picture, and what is the boundary between it and civic obligation? If you are willing to go to one extreme or the other, the answer is fairly simple. If the state is ultimate, then it commands and a man obeys whether it seems right in his eyes or not. Like an authoritarian church, a totalitarian state assumes the right to demand complete obedience; and it does not recognize the right of private judgment. On the other hand, if a man assumes that all his choices are his own responsibility and he owes nothing to society, the way becomes clear. Anarchy has the advantage of being logical at least, and one's acceptance of it is the end of tension when it comes to assuming any responsibility for society.

But most of us find ourselves somewhere in

between the extremes of this matter as well as in most of the issues. For Christianity at least one thing is clear, and that is that each man must respect a higher authority than the state. To fail to do that turns the government into a god and makes a mockery of religion and true worship. The state must pass laws for the guidance of its citizens, and then it must make provisions for the man whose conscience will not let him kill.

Many people become impatient with what they call the coddling of conscientious objectors to war. Why should exceptions be made, they ask; and why not demand the same obedience and conformity from each man? In times of crisis this point of view becomes powerful, and waves of hysteria sweep over a nation engulfing even the civil rights guaranteed by the Constitution. It is easy for people to become ruthless in dealing with the poor fellow who cannot obey the law for conscience' sake.

But the reason a state must recognize a higher authority than its own will is that without this recognition it turns into tyranny. This tyranny in turn becomes weakness and corruption, because when men have their consciences violated, they become hypocrites or martyrs or potential traitors. It is a law of history that societies which

60

deny the spiritual dignity of men are heading toward their doom.

The greatness of our country has been its understanding of this basic principle. Our laws take into account the man who is sincerely unable to do what the majority are willing to do. This has been not weakness but strength, and the denial of this philosophy is a frightening development. An inordinate concern with Communism, which is never defined with any preciseness, leads us to betray ourselves in the name of security.

There is an anecdote which has gone around among the peoples caught between American and Russian pressures. It seems that a certain Asian government cabled a Latin-American government to send it two Communists at once. The Latin Americans thought this was a strange request and cabled back, "Why?"

"Because," came the answer, "we have no Communists, and we cannot get American aid until we have some."[7]

We do wrong to assume that it makes no difference what we do or become in order to win the struggle. It is most necessary to be aware at all times of the difference between our world and

[7] Stringfellow Barr, *Citizens of the World* (New York: Doubleday & Co., Inc., 1952), p. 70.

theirs. It is most important that we remember that in our system man is first, and the legitimate purpose of a government is to serve rather than to be served. It is, in a word, the necessity of holding before our eyes the awful fact of God before whom every man and every nation must bow.

3. Real Problems Personal

A college under the control of a small, fundamentalist sect advertised that its campus was seven miles from any known form of sin. That would be a good trick if you could do it. If I believed that there was such a college, I would apply immediately for a job on the faculty; and if that were not forthcoming, I would settle for a job on the custodian's staff. There are few things I would be unwilling to do in order to get seven miles from sin. But because sin is in my heart and no one is able to tell me how to get seven miles from myself, the whole idea is futile. It is in the heart that a man has to face the great issues of his life.

We do not think that this is true, no matter how many times we hear it nor how often we give it a superficial assent. It still seems to us that our problems are caused by external affairs and their solutions are to be discovered in changing an outer environment. It is a part of the spirit of the time, and it roots in a materialistic civilization which bombards us constantly with materialistic values. If we could get out of our present job and take that more successful man's place, we think we would be all right. But too often, when we get to know that man, we discover that he carries burdens heavier than ours. We think that if we could live in a bigger house on a more elegant avenue, our worries would flee. Or if we could increase our income so that the end of each month would not find us trying to decide why the budget is out of balance, we believe life would run smoothly. It is our popular assumption that there is no human problem which cannot be solved by a more comfortable economic status.

The man who conducted a question-and-answer column in a Detroit newspaper made an interesting observation some time ago. He discovered that an encyclopedia published in 1768 allowed four lines for the word "atom" and five pages for the word "love." But in that same encyclopedia's latest edition five pages were given to "atom," and the word "love" did not occur at all. Which is a parable of the times! Atoms can be split to release physical power, but love is of the spirit, and therefore we assume that it is not of primary importance. We have gone all out in an attempt to reduce human life to physical things, but the condition of the world and the emptiness in men's hearts and minds do not testify to our success.

A most signficant phenomenon of this present time is the unhappiness of the successful. John D. Rockefeller once told his Sunday-school class: "It is wrong to assume that men of immense wealth are always happy." Every minister and counselor has learned that success is no guarantee of peace of mind, nor is wealth any defense against heartache. As a matter of fact, it has seemed to me that the man or woman who has gained all that our materialistic cleverness can provide for contentment is of all people most miserable. It is a terrible moment when one awakens to the truth that all his striving and sacrifice have left him with spiritual yearnings which mock his success. The great disillusionment comes to this generation when the promises of power prove empty and futile.

On the other hand, one is surprised constantly to learn of the happiness of the unsuccessful. How many families without all the comfort their neighbors enjoy have a kind of bubbling joy of the spirit that is above price? It is amazing to note the men and women whose lives flow into a simple pattern and yet who achieve the happiness their more ambitious brethren seek in vain. I have been a pastor long enough to cease being overly impressed by wealth and position, because too often they cover the life of quiet desperation. I have learned also to withhold my pity from the humble and the poor until I see whether or not they are rich in treasure which the world can neither give nor take away.

The meaning of all this is simply that pleasant surroundings and financial security are nice things to have, but they do not deal with the real problems of being human. The rich men who find contentment find it in their giving and sharing. They develop their gift for friendship, and they live with their families under the law of love. The ultimate questions are personal, which is to say they are spiritual. When dealing with persons, we are in the realm of absolutes. He who would speak for God speaks to the heart of man's mystery which lies deep down in the spiritual depths of his life.

My job makes it necessary for me to travel considerably, and I spend a certain amount of time on airplanes. There seems to be something about flying, especially at night, that makes it easier for people to talk about themselves to a stranger. Some of my best pastoral work is done on long flights in the night. A man may be sitting next to me with a burden that is too heavy for him to carry alone any longer. Perhaps he got on at Los Angeles and is going to Europe via New York. I will be leaving the airplane at Chicago, and he says to himself, "I'll never see this fellow again anyway, and—who knows?—perhaps he has some word for me." Then he will begin by saying, "I'm worried about my boy. Now don't misunderstand me; he is a good kid, and his mother and I have given him the best home any youngster could have. But he is running around with bad company, and we can't talk like we used to. What do you think about this younger generation?" Or sometimes a man wants to talk about the unhappiness at home, a coming divorce, or a business failure. But practically never does a person want to talk about Eisenhower, or Congress, or world affairs. He wants to find help for his personal problem, which is always in the realm of the spirit. For when a man is wrong spiritually, he is wrong in all his life; and nothing can cover that failure. God is a spirit, and the spirit of man is God's candle. Let the spokesman for God remember that!

4. Answers from God

A. J. Cronin in his autobiography, *Adventures in Two Worlds,* gives this testimony:

> I have come also to acknowledge the great illusion which lies in the pursuit of a purely material goal. What slight satisfaction lies in temporal honour and worldly grandeur! ... All the material possessions for which I strove so strenuously mean less to me now than a glance of love from those who are dear to me.
>
> Above all am I convinced of the need, irrevocable and inescapable, of every human heart, for God. No matter how we try to escape, to lose ourselves in restless seeking, we cannot separate ourselves from our divine source. There is no substitute for God.[8]

Our great error is in assuming that God is our refuge only for special times and for certain problems. We repeat the blasphemy of Ahaz, who became enamored with a pagan altar in Damascus and ordered the priest Urijah to have a replica made for the Temple in Jerusalem. This became the center for the nation's worship, and all the important sacrifices were made on it. But he was not willing to discard entirely the little brazen altar which had stood formerly in the honored place for sacrifices unto God. He put it on the north side, and, as he said to Urijah, he

[8] New York: McGraw-Hill Book Co., Inc., 1952, p. 328. Used by permission of the publisher.

would offer the important sacrifices on the great altar, but the little altar would be for him to inquire by.

It has been the tragic foolishness of our time to assume that life can be centered around paganism and religion kept in the background to be used for the special crises. We would like to believe that we can turn to God for help in the hour of trouble and darkness, but when things seem to go well and we are not frightened, then we can live as if he did not reign. But whether we recognize it or not, he reigns and his laws operate continually and forever.

We are in need of some influence to persuade us that it is in God that we live and move and have our being. Our split lives can find no wholeness until they are made whole again by him. Deep in the consciousness of man there is this expectancy and faith that God will speak to him because God made him. A missionary in Africa tried to describe to an old chief who Jesus was and what kind of person he had come to represent. The old man, who had never heard a previous word on Christianity, said thoughtfully, "Yes, I know him; I have heard his voice in the treetops at night." Another missionary, fleeing before the invading Japanese, found himself in a little village in China. He carried on his evangelistic work, and after he had described his Lord, an old woman replied, "I have always felt there was such a One, but no one could tell me His name." [9] It has been the experience of more than one preacher that a man who had never been within the church life seemed already convinced in his heart that some day someone would surely come and tell him about the kind of God Jesus revealed.

The spokesman for God can speak his word with the confidence that every man will know already something of what he has to tell. We do not speak of some extra thing which men have to be convinced they need badly enough to buy. As Sherwood Anderson said, Americans do not buy things; they are sold. This has been too often the attitude of the world toward religion, and religious spokesmen have been willing too often to accept the idea that they must sell God to men. Not so! Deep crieth unto deep, and the spirit of man cries to God, who is a Spirit. I never grow weary of watching a congregation sing the hymn

> O God, our help in ages past,
> Our hope for years to come,

[9] Carlyle Marney, *These Things Remain* (New York and Nashville: Abingdon Press, 1953), p. 51.

Our shelter from the stormy blast,
And our eternal home!

It seems to me always that one can see men saying to themselves with a kind of wonder, "Why of course this is true! What a fool I have been to seek refuge somewhere else!"

It is fine to read the strong, fearless words of the prophets when they called their people back to God. Listen to Isaiah: "Fear not, thou worm Jacob, and ye men of Israel; I will help thee saith the Lord, and thy redeemer, the Holy One of Israel" (41:14 K.J.V.). It is true that when men are afraid, they cease to be men and sink into an animal category. Isaiah says they become worms, but they can be saved if they commit their fear unto God. Fear is a spiritual matter, and its healing is a spiritual process.

The glory of the religious experience comes not only to men who make the first move in reaching up to grasp God's hand. There is yet another depth in the experience, when a man feels God's hand grasping his. It is like the small boy who was hurrying through a crowd clinging desperately to his father's hand as he had been told to do. But finally he gasped out, "I'm too tired to hang on any longer. You will have to hang onto me." When we get rid of our pride and confess our weakness, then there comes the One who lays hold of us when our strength is at an end.

Let him who speaks for God assume that men are longing for God even when they are not aware of it. While it is true that men flee from what they truly seek, soon or late they must exhaust every other search and turn to him. A Sunday-school class of small boys learned that one of their members was to have a birthday. They planned a surprise party for him and arrived on the appointed day. The boy's mother called him because she was sure he was not far away, but he did not answer, and he could not be found. Finally they went ahead with the games, ate the cake and the ice cream, and left for home without the guest of honor making an appearance. Later he came home, and his mother persisted until she had the truth. He had heard her call all right, but supposing that she had an errand or a job for him, he had run away until suppertime. Jesus told a story about a man who prepared a dinner, and no one would come. It is a part of our human perversity that we are afraid to trust God's gracious invitation. But our spirits cannot be content, for they were made for fellowship with him. When we speak to the spiritual nature of man, we speak for God.

III

Who Speaks for Freedom!

Is not this the fast that I choose:
to loose the bonds of wickedness,
to undo the thongs of the yoke,
to let the oppressed go free,
and to break every yoke?
—Isa. 58 :6

For freedom Christ has set us free; stand fast therefore, and do not submit again to a yoke of slavery. —Gal. 5 :1

THE INDIAN PHILOSOPHER RADHAKRISHNAN WAS interviewed some time ago regarding his attitude toward the East, the West, and the present tension. Among other things he said this: "I firmly believe that man will endure and triumph; that the quality of all religions depends upon their power to make men more free, not to fill them with fear and hate; upon the power of their advocacy of love, not hate; of faith, not doubt." [1] Thus does one of the greatest contemporary voices of the East proclaim that the measure of a religion is a measure of its power to release

[1] *The Saturday Review*, June 27, 1953, p. 37.

72

men. In the long, long history of man's seeking for God, there are any number of instances where religions have played the part of slavery and not freedom. As a matter of fact, any faith tends to fall into the hands of a hierarchy which would use it as a means of setting limits to the minds and spirits of men. It would be a good thing for each man to remember that unless his own religion sets him free and promises freedom to all men, it is weighed and found wanting.

Christians would do well to look at their faith in the light of freedom. They would do well to remember that Jesus set forth the purpose of his ministry in his home town of Nazareth. Being in the synagogue on the Sabbath, as was his custom, he was invited to speak. He used as the text of his sermon these words of Isaiah:

The Spirit of the Lord is upon me,
because he has anointed me to preach the good news to the
    poor.
He has sent me to proclaim release to the captives
and recovering of sight to the blind,
to set at liberty those who are oppressed,
to proclaim the acceptable year of the Lord. (Luke 4:18-19.)

Whenever religion has been at its best, it has exemplified this spirit of the prophet; and it has

73

been the enemy of every force that would narrow man's mind or confine his spirit.

Religious men have insisted always that this is the main purpose of government. A good many years ago Spinoza wrote: "The ultimate aim of government is not to rule, or restrain by fear, nor to exact obedience, but contrariwise, to free every man from fear. . . . In fact, the true aim of government is liberty." Which is to say that every institution of human society for the good of man is for his liberty, and every institution which is evil in human society has as its aim his enslavement. In whatever realm it may be, we have a criterion of a man's authority if we simply ask whether or not he speaks for freedom. If the answer is "no," then we may be sure he is speaking against God. If the answer is "yes," we will expect to hear the accent of the Eternal in such a man's speech. He who speaks for God speaks for freedom.

1. Freedom Not License

The common mistake of our generation has been to confuse freedom with license. Whenever we have talked about being free, we have thought it meant doing just as we pleased without rules or regulations to limit or embarrass us. Freedom has been defined as absence of authority, and we have tried to go back to a period described by the Book of Judges as a time when each man did what was right in his own eyes. It is amazing how many crimes are committed and how many sins against one's fellows are condoned, all in the name of personal liberty.

Our revolt against authority has led us into the world of a relativism where it is assumed that everything is to be decided in accordance with its immediate profit. That is, we have said that it is wrong if you do it, but it is right if I do it because I have a legitimate reason; or it is wrong today, but it may be right tomorrow under different circumstances. Thus we have come to look upon all ethical behavior as simply that kind of action which serves our present desires. While we have been properly shocked at this when carried to its extreme by the cynical Communists, we have been quite willing to practice it more quietly under the covering of democracy. But somehow after the first excitement of throwing off the restraint has ended, we find ourselves lost and groping.

In the realm of morals our insistence on license is supposed to lead us back to a more natural life. If man is only an animal, then he should live like animals; and the struggle to get rid of conscience has been one of our most eager philosophical enterprises. We have laughed at old moral codes as if they were things which went with the styles of dress of a bygone period, and we have felt smug and complacent in our own lack of restraint.

When license becomes our goal, then all social responsibility comes to an end. Selfishly we seek that which serves our own cause without too much thought of the effect upon other people. The success philosophy, which assumes that all will be forgiven if you succeed, is the ruling passion of a large segment of the population. It has become a commonplace to assume that a man's service to the community should wait until he has firmly established his own fortune. The Ten Commandments seem to us to be not words from God thundered down from Sinai, but opinions of an ancient and limited people, to be discussed perhaps, but not to be taken too seriously. When Edwin McNeill Poteat refers to them as a "mandate to humanity," it sounds to this contemporary generation extreme and exaggerated.

A minister was talking to some young people and comparing their lives to a football game, which may be trite but is always a popular way of reaching the minds of youth. He went on to tell them how the game should be played with

76

honesty and bravery, and worked up to what he thought was a very fine climax. It was rather spoiled, however, by a boy who said, "But we do not even know where the goal posts are." [2] The strange truth comes home to us at last that the game has no meaning unless there are goals and limitations. If a man is supposed to play according to his own ideas and follow only his own inclinations, then no game is possible. Something seems to have gone wrong in all this mad pursuit of liberty. It seemed so fine as we started on the path, but somehow we have arrived at a dead end; and we must painfully retrace our steps to discover where we took the wrong turning.

The results of this license in society are fairly apparent if we have eyes to see. While we try to explain our debacle in more shallow terms, the truth is that underneath it we reveal the tragedy of a generation that sought freedom and found emptiness. Into this vacuum there have come men to fill it with their own ambitions and their own authority. They were the ones who taught a new generation that the great word is not truth but obedience. But this would have been impossible unless men were so sick and tired of emptiness

[2] N. G. Long, *Goal Posts* (Atlanta: Tupper & Love, Inc., 1953), Foreword.

that they were willing to accept almost any evil nonsense to fill the void.

Mussolini many years ago remarked that the truth apparent to everyone was that men had grown weary of liberty. He used the wrong word actually, and he should have said "license," for that is what it was. We did not believe that he was right, and we could not understand that nations would deliberately choose slavery for freedom. We failed to understand that men would rather be slaves than be victims of their own empty despair. They will obey something and if not God then the tyrant. While we have hoped that this madness was confined to a particular section of the world and it certainly could not happen here, it becomes more and more apparent that we are not so different from our brethren abroad as we thought. The possibility that a generation nurtured in a democracy cut off from its spiritual roots could turn reactionary, is far from impossible.

All of us must be troubled by the mystery of otherwise brilliant men having been attracted to Communism, even in the United States. What happened to these intellectuals that they accepted all the confinement and blind obedience demanded by such a system? As I have read their testimony, especially the ones who have repented and returned to the democratic fold again, I have been impressed with the loneliness which drove them to their enslavement. Read the confessions of men who wrote chapters in *The God that Failed,* or read *Witness* by Whittaker Chambers. So many of them tell us that they were isolated, unrelated, and Communism promised them fellowship and purpose.

Jesus could have been talking straight to us when he described the empty house and the evil spirits. Listen again to his words:

When the unclean spirit has gone out of a man, he passes through waterless places seeking rest; and finding none he says, "I will return to my house from which I came." And when he comes he finds it swept and put in order. Then he goes and brings seven other spirits more evil than himself, and they enter and dwell there; and the last state of that man becomes worse than the first. (Luke 11:24-26.)

It is not enough to cleanse one's life from an evil spirit, and it is never enough just to drive out slavery. If the house remains empty, other spirits come back to fill it; and they are more evil than the first ones. We must come to terms with this truth about ourselves, namely, that emptiness of spirit means disaster.

Michael Faraday says that when he was a boy,

he sold newspapers. One day while waiting for his papers in front of the iron gates of the newspaper office, he put his arms and head through the bars. His already scientifically inclined mind began to analyze the situation. With his arms and head on one side of the gate and his heart and body on the other side, on which side was the real Michael Faraday? He says that at this point someone opened the gate and nearly jerked his head off, so that he learned quickly that there is no profit in trying to be on both sides at the same time. One has to take his stand and pay the price, which is better than the destruction which comes to those seeking neutrality in this battle of living.

We do not need to look at this merely in terms of nations, for it comes close to us in the individuals about us, perhaps even in ourselves. I am troubled by the essential tawdriness and uselessness of so many lives in our time. This is not apparent from the outside, for a man may pose as fairly successful, and perhaps economically he is. But let him stop for a little while and consider himself and talk to someone honestly. A long drifting has landed him on no island where he wanted to be. While he tries to prevent its happening very often, now and again there breaks upon him the haunting suspicion that perhaps his life is not worth living and it has no longer real meaning nor dignity. This is the specter which haunts the masses of our generation—the specter of meaninglessness. We are supposed to be free, but we do not know what we are free for. The tension seems to have snapped and left us unstrung and useless. This is all the more alarming when we consider that the greater success we have had in attaining what we thought was freedom, the more dissatisfied we are. The trouble of course is in our definition. We have gone wrong in assuming that freedom is license; it is not.

G. K. Chesterton, one of the great and original Christian writers, was also one of the most absent-minded of men. He had difficulty in keeping his dates straight, and he never could remember the schedule of a lecture tour. A friend one time received a wire, reply paid, "Am I coming to you tonight, or what?" The friend had to reply, "Not this Tuesday but next Wednesday." But perhaps the most famous case of his confusion was this telegram he sent to his wife, "Am in Market Harborough. Where ought I to be?" She replied, "Home;" because, as she said later, it was easier to get him home and start him off again on the right track than to tell him how to get where he ought to be from where he was. So it is with us.

We are here, but where ought we to be? If only someone could tell us to come home and start us off again on the right track. But in our confusion we do not even know the direction of home.

2. Freedom—Responsibility and Discipline

We must come back to the realization that to be free does not mean license, but it means finding the laws of our being and obeying them. Freedom is not the removal of authority but the discovering of the real authority. It is not the absence of discipline, but it is finding the discipline which will make us able to enter into our inheritance and accomplish our destiny. It is, in a word, discovery of that framework of law which God has provided for men to live by.

There are any number of instances of this in the world round about us, if we have eyes to see. If a ship were sailed under the philosophy of license, it would be a sorry spectacle indeed. Stay away from the rudder and let the sails fall slack and flap about in the wind as they will. You may be sure that the voyage will be a short one with the ship wallowing in the troughs of the waves until she goes down. But let someone who knows about these things keep the sails taut with the wind; put a hand upon the tiller and keep her on the course; then as she sweeps down the bay, we look and say the ship sails free. We say it because this is what the ship was made for by the builder. There are few sights more beautiful than a yacht sailing free before the wind. We can hardly escape the feeling that if the ship could speak, she would rejoice that under discipline she is not a victim of the wind and the wave but, in a sense, master of them both.

A man who watches the professional golfer has the impression that golf is the simplest and easiest game in the world, for there is nothing to it except relaxation and smooth motion. If someone says to him that back of the professional's skill there is long, hard work and many years of practice, he might reply that it cannot be so; he will not believe it. He will be a golfer himself, and he will pay no attention to the rules and regulations, because the game is obviously for free men. He will discover, however, that the smoothness of motion is the result of discipline; and if he expects to have something of the joy which comes to the expert, he will have to accept the responsibility which such a status puts upon the player. Every athlete who has become expert in his field always gives the impression of effortless rhythm and grace. But the man who takes his exercise in the bleachers has only to try the game for himself to discover that an athlete's freedom is a very costly affair.

The owning of a home had been a dream of ours for many a long year. Finally it became possible not only to own a home but to have one built. It was a great experience. We had assumed that one just decided what was wanted, told the architect to draw the plans, and hired a builder to follow the instructions. It is not so simple. Beside the limitation of cost, there is the limitation of space and material. There are some things you just cannot do, and there are some combinations you just cannot have. If you choose this, then you must give up that, until in one moment of weary disappointment my wife remarked that having a house built was simply choosing the lesser of two evils. It is not quite that bad actually, but it does demand choice and the responsibility of deciding what comes first. One has to come to terms with things as they are and accept the limitations of the possible. Building, like so much of life, seems to be a matter of carefully weighing the advantages and the disadvantages without ever experiencing a situation where everything is advantages only.

A certain village drunkard was hauled into court regularly. Finally the judge asked, "How with all this drunkenness do you manage to support yourself?"

The drunk replied, "Well, usually I lean against a fence."

But life has a way of removing the fence and insisting that we stand on our own feet and come to terms with responsibility and discipline. If we refuse, we might find something to lean against for a while but not for long. Freedom costs something, and the efforts which freedom demands are sometimes so great that we flee from them. We hope in vain that there is an easier way to enjoy liberty.

Men are free when they are masters of themselves, which is to say, when they have disciplined themselves. If some habit, which we cannot break, has control over us, then we are foolish to talk about being free men. We may argue about this habit for long weary hours and do our best to persuade ourselves that it is really not very wrong, because so many other people are doing it. But something tells us that this is not for us, and we wish we could break it. Until somehow we reach out and find the power which helps us to destroy it, we are slaves; and we know it. Whenever we would come into the presence of God or whenever we try to pray, there stands before us this barrier of our slavery;

and we cannot reach him and he cannot reach us. Whenever the physical desires of our body become so unruly that our minds cannot control them, then our appetites become our masters. But the man who has a disciplined body and who uses the physical equipment which God has given him to serve the higher purposes of the soul knows that he has entered into the experience of true freedom.

Men are free when they are masters of their fear. There may be something which frightens us even when we are afraid to admit it to ourselves, and we are haunted by this slavery which never allows us any quietness of heart. More people than we know are haunted by some secret dread which they have not dared to share with anyone else and which they hesitate to face openly. In some cases it has not been defined with any clearness at all, but it is there hiding behind their brave masks. Sooner or later it has to be faced and conquered, if they are to live as men ought to live.

Men are not free when they are afraid of ideas. This is a particularly prevalent kind of fear today, and it has been carried to ridiculous extremes in our society. The very suspicion that here is a new interpretation or a concept that may not be entirely orthodox sends shivers of fright down the spines of reactionists. There seems to be the strange idea that if we can just keep any new experiment or any new suggestion out of our thinking and speaking, we will be safe. Orthodoxy becomes our idol and conventionality our creed. There has grown up the assumption that if a man should talk to a Communist, it would mean automatically that he is in danger of becoming a Communist. The radical idea that Democracy is stronger than Communism seems to be too much for our fearful time. We would keep our children in ignorance rather than inform them of the weaknesses and the evil which result from this other way of life. It is a time that demands free men, which is to say men who are not afraid to examine their own affirmations as well as the affirmations of the enemy.

There are some religious men who tremble at every new discovery of science or every unorthodox concept of God. They are afraid that their faith will be destroyed, and they act as if they carry the weight of their religion upon their shoulders. Great religion is not a burden to men, but wings for their spirits. We do not carry it so much as it carries us. If we have taken the responsibility of following the discipline of careful thought and spiritual honesty, then we will not be afraid of the new ideas men may announce.

The truth is that freedom is faith, and the man who has discovered liberty of soul and mind is the one who has beat out on the anvil of experience his own beliefs and his own creed. Having tested his faith at every turn and ventured out into the dangerous places of life with it, he is not afraid of the competition of the open market place. It is the man who has tried to come by liberty too easily who is uncertain and suspicious. If we have earned our right to be free, we will glory in it and live by it.

Oliver Wendell Holmes set down a famous dissenting opinion in the Abrams' case in 1919:

But when men have realized that time has upset many fighting faiths, they may come to believe even more than they believe the very foundations of their own conduct that the ultimate good desired is better reached by free trade in ideas—that the best of truth is the power of the thought to get itself accepted in the competition of the market, and that truth is the only ground upon which their wishes safely can be carried out. That at any rate is the theory of our Constitution. It is an experiment, as all life is an experiment. Every year if not every day we have to wager our salvation upon some prophecy based upon imperfect knowledge. While that experiment is part of our system I think that we should be eternally vigilant against attempts to check the expression of opinions that we loathe and believe to be fraught with death, unless they so imminently threaten immediate interference with the lawful and pressing purposes of the law that an immediate check is required to save the country.

The great jurist was saying essentially that we live by faith and that free men are not afraid to have their faith tested in the fires of daily living. For underneath our freedom there has to be the confidence that truth must be the ultimate goal of men and that truth always has the final word. If our responsibility is to truth and our lives are disciplined in such a way as to desire that above all else, then, and then only, are we truly free men.

Charles Francis Potter relates that in one of his pastorates his parsonage was located in a rather well-to-do section of the city. His salary, however, did not measure up to the neighborhood, so that his children lacked the expensive toys the sons of wealthier neighbors enjoyed. They referred to his youngsters as the "five-and-ten kids." But they were not to be intimidated, so they formed a club and transformed the backyard of the parsonage into a boys' paradise with tents, caves, and shacks. Every afternoon strange youngsters from other neighborhoods came to play with them, and these young Irish and Italians had a great time while the poor little rich boys gathered on the outside and

wished that they might participate. One day one
of these sons of wealth asked four-year old Myron
Potter if he could not join the club. Myron
ordered him to turn around and then said deliberately, "No, go on home. No boy can belong
to this club unless he has patches on his pants." [3]
So it is that in the society of free men no man
belongs who does not have the marks of sacrifice
and the scars of battle. It is not for the soft, the
pampered, nor the favored. It is for men who
have wrought out their faith through struggle
and have found their freedom by accepting responsibility for truth and disciplining their lives
to become fit instruments of free spirits.

3. Freedom's Need to Grow and Be Shared

It is interesting to note that so many of the
clear insights regarding the nature of our American democracy come to us from outsiders. One
of the most alert of observers was Alexis de
Tocqueville, a French student of political
systems. He said one time: "Despots themselves
do not deny that freedom is excellent; only they
desire it for themselves alone, and they maintain
that everyone else is altogether unworthy of it.
Thus it is not about the value of freedom that we

[3] *The Preacher and I* (New York: Crown Publishers, Inc., 1951).
p. 116.

differ, but about the value greater or smaller that we set on mankind.''

It is here that we reach a stumbling block in our thinking. It is true that we want to be free individually and personally, but we hesitate sometimes to agree that this same freedom should be given to all men. We may be willing to share it with a few, especially if they live on our street and they are our kind. But that what we are asking for ourselves has to belong to every man, regardless of his race or status, is a hard saying. Yet if we look at it very carefully, we come to the conclusion that we have no real choice in this matter. If we try to keep it for ourselves, we lose it; and our only safety is in sharing it with everyone around the world. Freedom has to grow or it dies; it has to be shared or it withers. History is full of instances of classes who discovered this truth too late and lost what they had because they could not keep it to themselves alone. There is no place where we can see more clearly the truth of Jesus' admonition that if we are to save our lives, we must lose them than in this matter of freedom.

Elmer Davis wrote a very significant article with this title, ''Are We Worth Saving?'' [4] He

4 *Harper's Magazine*, Aug., 1953, pp. 23-30.

tried to analyze the meaning of our Western civilization to see if there was anything unique in it which needed to be preserved. He assumed that we are facing a struggle to the death, and if we are to make sacrifices for the preservation of our way, we must be sure that there is something in it worth the cost. He came to the conclusion that the fundamental value of our way is an assumption that all men have the right to think, to question, and to investigate. It is, in a word, freedom of the mind and freedom of experimentation for all, that constitutes the unique contribution of the West. G. F. Hudson has observed that "to repudiate faith in freedom is to abandon Western civilization." If this is true, and I think it is, then we must understand that what would be an absolute denial of all we stand for is fear of thought. It would be a sad thing, indeed, if in the name of preserving our civilzation we should deny the very value which makes it unique. It would be a tragedy if suddenly we drew back from the implications of our faith.

The indivisibility of freedom is something which we take a long time to learn. It is hard for us to comprehend that it belongs to all or to none. Some years ago I had an example of one group's comprehension of this principle which has lifted up my heart ever since. I was attending a Chinese student conference at Lake Tahoe at the time the Japanese were being moved from the Pacific Coast. One might have assumed that if any would be unconcerned with the fate of the Japanese, it would have been these Chinese students. For years the Japanese had been invaders of their homeland, and some of them had relatives and families who had suffered the misfortunes of this unprovoked attack. Their own people were putting up a desperate fight to maintain their independence, while the ruthlessness of the Japanese military machine had become a scandal around the world. Yet when the resolutions committee gave its report at the close of the conference, it contained a resolution championing the rights of the nisei as American citizens and criticizing the deportation. It was pointed out by the committee that whenever the rights of any minority are overridden, the rights of all minorities are in danger. I have thought about that a great deal since. If you want freedom for yourself, you must have freedom for all; and whenever or wherever it is attacked, it has to be defended then and there. This should be done, of course, because we are all brothers and have concern for one another. But if by any

93

chance we cannot measure up to that high insight, then let us know that for the protection of our own freedoms we have to be champions of freedom for all.

The history of the Civil Liberties Union has been a very interesting one, as well as a very confusing one to some people. That such an organization should be concerned about liberty for certain groups is clear enough; that it should be concerned about liberty for all groups is very hard to comprehend. Thus if you read the history of this amazing organization, you discover that it has fought for the rights of racial minorities, religious minorities, and political minorities of all kinds. It has sometimes championed the liberties of Communists and sometimes the liberties of Fascists. It has even provided legal aid for people whose professed philosophy has been a denial of the rights of all individuals. From this we can learn a much-needed lesson, which is that we must champion freedom of "expression of opinions that we loathe," as Justice Holmes put it.

This of course is our Protestant heritage, and one of the Reformation's lasting affirmations was its insistence that the Church is a wide, free fellowship and not an authoritarian organization. There are times when we wonder whether or not this idea is worth all the risk which is involved in it. We see strange little groups trying to make one small part of the gospel the whole gospel, attacking everyone else as if they were outside the communion of the saved. When we leave these matters of religion to the individual conscience, we get some very weird results. It is tragic indeed that Protestants have sometimes betrayed their own principle, as when John Calvin had Servetus burned at the stake for heresy on October 27, 1553. It is no comfort to the man who suffered the agony of the flames that nearly four hundred years later a monument was raised to his honor and to our shame. But it is of the greatest significance that our principle of individual freedom would bring us to a confession of our sin and I trust to a true and hearty repentance.

There are times when we wonder if our Catholic brethren are not wiser than we, taking care of the matter of creed, doctrine, and truth by means of a hierarchy which hands down its conclusions to the people. Yet a freedom which is only partial soon disappears and so easily turns into sham and dogma. It is therefore no accident that the great countries which have produced democracy have been almost without exception Protestant countries, where every man's right to be free in his worship has been written into the constitution. At the end of the day we believe it is better to take this risk even though it leads us down some very strange paths and to some very dubious conclusions. If the priesthood of all believers means paths which lead off on a tangent, it means also the foundation of liberty. Men whose worship becomes automatic and thoughtless cannot have their lives very deeply influenced thereby. The immediate advantages of authority are dissipated by the long-term testing which shows up the real toughness of universal, individual liberty.

A Latin-American woman from a wealthy family was asked how things were going in her country. She replied that things were going very badly indeed, because even the cooks wanted to send their sons to the university. What a typical reaction that is! That the sons of some families should go to the university would be admitted gladly if the privileges could be limited to those who are superior socially. And in the minds of some people it becomes a scandal when ordinary folk want the same privilege for their sons. But in some strange way it is true that either you have to accept it for everybody or you cannot keep it for anyone.

That this hunger for liberty has certain dangers connected with it can never be denied. Once you begin to share liberty with people, you never know how far it will go or how they may use it. Abraham Lincoln faced this fact in the days of the Civil War when he was urged to hold back and wait. His assumption that this country cannot exist half slave and half free was never thoroughly accepted in the North any more than it was in the South. The ideal was all well enough as long as it could be held as an ideal, but when the time came actually to put it into practice, many a man drew back and decided that he had not meant to carry it quite so far.

We face that same situation in our world to-day. We have talked for a long time about all nations becoming free and all men having the opportunities which we possess. We have had no trouble in talking about it as if we understood it, but now that the time has come actually to accept it, many of us draw back in consternation. In place of a well-ordered world where some sections are colonies under the control of the stronger nations of the West, we suddenly look into revolution and independence movements, which mean not stability but unrest. Too late now to realize that much of this desire for freedom came from us, at least from our pronouncements and from our missionaries. It seems in some ways that we are getting more than we bargained for, and if it were possible, we would draw back to a safer world where some peoples are free and others are not. But it is too late now, and it was only a question of time anyway until we had to face the truth that freedom will not be bound.

We might do well to look at the risk God took when he made men free. That was the first great experiment and the first great affirmation of faith. If we can understand the mind of God at all, we must thrill at his willingness to release men from the limitations of the animal world and give them the right to seek and rebel. The risk God took is the risk we must take, for there is no other way for men to grow and increase their wisdom except they have liberty of mind and spirit. In our time we may try to hold back, but it will do no good, and it will only lose us the leadership of the world. For even as God took the great risk of making men free, he makes it necessary for men to take the risk of bringing freedom to their brothers and finally entering into that kingdom where tyranny is no more.

After Disraeli had been elevated to the peerage, he found it very difficult to attend the Cabinet meetings because of illness. Yet in spite of the warnings regarding his health he continued to go whenever it was possible because, as he said, "One must run risks in life, or else it would be as dull as death." [5] Life is full of risks, and freedom is one of its greatest. But it is only by taking the risk gladly and understanding that God wills it that the new heaven and the new earth can be approached. Speak for God! Speak for freedom!

4. Freedom Rooted in God

The great textbook of liberty is the Bible, for from beginning to end it is the story of God's attempt to set people free. He tries to free them from their enemies but particularly from themselves. This was the burden of the prophet's message, and even the Law was a framework within which man's spirit might attain its true liberty. It is the burden of the message of the Old Testament prophets that God purposes and wills that men should be released from every bond and every yoke which oppresses them. "The spirit of man is the lamp of the Lord, searching all his

[5] Hesketh Pearson, *Dizzy: The Life and Personality of Benjamin Disraeli* (New York: Harper & Bros., 1951), p. 258.

innermost parts." (Prov. 20:27.) The light of God in the heart of man is the source of his freedom, and the spirit of man is the candle of the Lord. After all is said and done, we come back to God as the source of man's meaning and the true source of his nature. Once we lose sight of this, we have lost sight of our credentials and our real authority. In the words of the old collect, it is God in whose service man finds perfect freedom.

The apostle Paul understood the high calling of Jesus as the releasing of power for man to win freedom from sin and self. In Paul's description of the Christian experience our Lord overcomes the barrier of the Law and by introducing a new and higher law of love, makes the final victory possible. This personal experience of Paul is the epitome of the story of mankind. Christianity is fulfilling its true service when it brings freedom to men and their societies. Its denial is a turning toward enslavement within and tyranny without. "For freedom Christ has set us free; stand fast therefore, and do not submit again to a yoke of slavery." (Gal. 5:1.)

The world seems to have as its main purpose the creation of free persons. The unhappiness of many people is produced by their assumption that the world exists to make them happy. If this is its purpose, then the world is certainly a failure; for there are too many tragic accidents which come to innocent folk. You would have a hard time convincing that mother whose boy was killed just sixteen minutes before the Korean truce was signed that the world exists primarily to make people happy. If we begin with this view of the world, we are bound to be disappointed and disillusioned before very long. We shall have no answer for the dark happenings and no faith to hold us steady when the evil times come.

No, the world seems to be made as a training ground for freedom. Whoever created our life here seems to have assumed that the final purpose should be great persons rather than happy ones. A life that produces character has to be full of risk and the possibility of tragedy. This does not mean that God deserts us in these hours, but that he leads us through the valley of the shadows to a higher fulfillment of our life. His Spirit enters into every human experience, and he walks beside us through pain and failure.

The whole matter of freedom is not something we can leave in the realm of choice, for it is a matter of absolute necessity. Men must be free, not because they prefer it but because God wills it. Even when men grow weary of their liberty, it is an obligation which has to be borne in order to achieve their status as sons of God. To assume that we have a choice in this matter is a false assumption which will lead us only into confusion. Today we cannot crawl back into the sea or into some hole and be secure. We are men, and we must walk the earth freely, for the future of humanity is at stake.

The divine judgment on any program, therefore, is the extent to which it brings freedom to men. No matter what promises a man may make or what rewards a cause may seem to guarantee, if it limits men, it is evil and must be destroyed. No matter how promising a speaker is, or how much he may resemble the Pied Piper of Hamlin, we shall know whether he speaks in the name of God once we determine whether he proposes liberty or slavery. The United Presbyterian General Assembly voiced the common religious faith at its session in June, 1953. It said: "We reaffirm our belief in the absolute necessity of freedom of religion. We fear, despise, and resist any tendency to coerce the religious conscience. . . . We believe religious liberty is the will of God."

Eric Sevareid was lost in the land of the headhunters when trying to fly the Hump between

Burma and China during World War II. A friend of his hiked into the hills with a heavy pack on his back to meet him. The pack was getting heavier when the friend met a native Naga boy. He resorted to pidgin English: "You coolie. Carry pack. Carry pack. Five mile. Give much rupee—much rupee." He jingled the coins in his pocket. "You help him white man, no?"

"No," replied the Naga boy gravely, "I am on my way to the Christian high school, and I am just as fatigued as you are."

Is that good, or is that bad? The weary man may have felt for the moment that it was bad, but in the long run he must come to understand that it was good, for until each man has a sense of his own worth, the true world of brotherhood can never be established. The Christian high school which gave that boy his feeling of equality and value was speaking the voice of God. We will not make the promise that freedom will always bring us comfort, and there are times when it may insist on less comfort for us that others may have their burdens lightened. But we insist that whatever the cost it is worth it, for God wills freedom for all his children.

Russell Criddle wrote an amazing story of what it means to be blind and then see again after a miraculous operation. After years of blindness one of the new operations was performed and a new eye cornea grafted. On the way to the home where he was staying in New York after the operation, he realized suddenly that he could see. This is what he wrote about it:

> Everything looked beautiful. Nothing looked ugly. The wad of paper in the gutter—the words alone convey an idea of filth, but I saw white, and black, and straight lines; color and symmetry unbelievably different from any other wad of paper in any other gutter.
>
> But after all there was the beauty of people. Some children were playing in the driveway. An old lady walked toward us, and passed. I felt no great thrill that I was no longer blind; only the awful sense of beauty thrilled me to the limit of endurance.
>
> I hurried into the house and to my room, and buried my head in the pillow. Not because I was no longer blind, not because I could see, but because I had not the capacity to digest so much grandeur. I wept.[6]

So too the man caught in the slavery of his own worst impulse or the victim of other men's lust for power comes out into the new freedom which Christ offers all men. It is like coming from darkness into light and from ugliness into beauty. For no matter how much slavery may be

[6] *Love Is Not Blind* (New York: W. W. Norton & Co., Inc., 1953), p. 260.

disguised, it is still darkness and confinement. But freedom comes like the rising of the sun in the morning and casts upon us the promise of new life and new hope. It is for all men, and he who speaks for freedom for himself and for his brethren speaks for God.

IV

Who Speaks for Hope!

For in this hope we were saved. Now hope that is seen is not hope. For who hopes for what he sees? But if we hope for what we do not see, we wait for it with patience. —Rom. 8:24-25

Return to your stronghold, O prisoners of hope; today I declare that I will restore to you double. —Zech. 9:12

CHRISTIANITY HAS ALWAYS BEEN THE OBJECT OF two common forms of criticism. It never seems to dawn on the critics that if one attack is valid, the other cannot be and that indeed if launched together, they cancel each other. Yet sometimes the same man will hold these two opinions at the same time. He will insist in the first place that Christianity is too hopeful about human nature and too optimistic concerning human destiny. It has not been an unusual thing in days past for the so-called realists to have a field day in this game. But just when one has made up his mind that Christianity must be a very sentimental philosophy, the same critic insists in the second place that it is too drab, too dour, and too demanding. Now the Christian faith is made to appear as a dampener of human spirits and a thief which steals away the joy of life. It looks at human nature too seriously, these critics now insist; and it takes life altogether too seriously. It seems strange that it is such a popular thing to attack the Christian faith as being at one and the same time too hopeful and not hopeful enough.

This could mean, of course, that Christianity has found the middle way and has refused to be forced either to the right or to the left. It could mean that there is always a real basis of hope even in the darkest situation, while at the same time there is cause for alarm on the very sunniest of days. A cloud no bigger than a man's hand may be discernible to Christian prophets and invisible to worldlings. It does seem that the gospel is always bringing into men's minds a neglected element and trying to balance a one-sided picture with another point of view.

A generation which finds so many things going wrong with it loses the ability to see the things which are going right with it. Men tend to move in cycles; everything is all right, or everything is all wrong; either the sun will never go down or the sun will never come up. So when the Christian gospel proclaims the good news of hope in a dark time, it is ridiculed as sentimental. When it talks about judgment coming in the good times, it is looked upon as a joy killer.

The truth is that Christianity has so much depth in it that it sails the sea somewhat like a submarine. Beneath the surface there is a calmness which is not affected by either storms or fair weather. It has been predicted by some scientists that in the future great passenger submarines will be developed to cross the sea and no one will get seasick. So Christianity is aware of a depth of living where the surface disturbances are not of ultimate significance. In the darkest times the man who speaks for God speaks for hope, which may be invisible to those who think the contemporary situation is an unchanging one. No philosophy regards hope as an imperative, but you may be sure that the man who speaks for God will have running through even his darkest prophecies the shining light of a mighty hope.

1. The Evil of a Shallow Optimism

Someone defined a pessimist as a fellow who has had to live with an optimist. There are few things in life more distressing than to be in the presence of one who is incapable of seriousness

even in the face of the most distressing situa-
tions. The congenitally optimistic individual is
probably better to have around than the one who
is constantly pessimistic. But not too much better, for a good healthy dose of doubt and questioning is necessary if one is to keep psycholog-
ically healthy. The constant dispenser of cheer is
one who fails to instill confidence, precisely because like the propagandist for any particular
point of view men begin to see that he has become
blind to the larger situation. Like any other individual with a single-track mind, his point of view
is discounted automatically, because he can see
life neither steadily nor whole. Such a man was
portrayed in Arthur Miller's *Death of a Sales-
man*. The hero made being well liked the end goal
of his life and awoke, when it was too late, to the
realization that he had merely made himself
ridiculous. We remember the pitiful service-club
luncheons during the depths of the depression,
when little groups of frightened men met together to sing songs and indulge in horseplay in
the hopes that if they ignored their fears, they
might go away.

But not only is this shallow optimism unrealistic; it is evil. The prophets of Israel found
themselves helpless until they could crack the
veneer of a false confidence which covered their

109

society. Amos, for example, had to smash the idea that being the chosen people guaranteed God's protection regardless of Israel's morals and ethics. The sweet singers who fill some of our pulpits and write so many of our books are not only misdirected men but seducers and betrayers. The beginning of many a man's salvation takes place when he can free himself from the attitude that something is bound to turn up. He needs to come face to face with the realization that nothing has turned up and probably never will unless he repents, which is to say, makes the painful decision to turn in another direction. The evil nature of false optimism needs to be faced.

It is evil for one thing, because misplaced optimism prevents the necessary action which would save us. We know it has happened to many nations, and the failure of a people to face the challenge and respond to it looms as one of the main causes of national decline. It is astounding to note how seldom a ruling group really understands the seriousness of political discontent. French noblemen still hoped up to the last minute that the French Revolution would pass over and have but a minor effect on this condition. The queen could make the whole business seem unimportant by suggesting that if the people had no bread to eat, then let them eat cake. Wealth and power find it so difficult to believe that poverty and weakness plus despair can shatter all the little barriers and march across the land like a devastation.

Before the Bolshevik revolution began to flame across Russia, the nobility went its way concerned chiefly with the minor matters of its own comfort. It awakened only when death came into the palaces and security proved to be an illusion of the imagination. Only a few men in England understood the seriousness of the discontent of the American colonists, and they were not strong enough to influence the government until it was too late. Looking back on the situation now, it seems incredible that England could have been so blind to the necessity of conciliation.

We take the same easygoing attitude toward our resources. Our forests can be cut as long as a fortune is being made; the soil can be plowed as long as there is a good price for wheat. Surely the floods will not come next year, and surely the dust bowl is so far in the future that we need not worry about it for at least a generation. The experts who warn what these things mean to a nation are silenced and fortunes are piled up, but the land is ruined, and the next generation is robbed of its heritage. Every man who speaks the accent of false optimism is not only mis-

111

taken, but bad. He prevents the people from facing up to the necessity of taking the action which can save them.

So far as the individual is concerned, he discovers that this tendency always to look on the bright side can be a very evil thing for his future. The enslaving power of the pleasant habit which begins to take hold of him throws out a warning now and then, but he ignores the signs and goes on until he cannot break the habit. He believes that somehow the damage which has happened to others cannot happen to him, and the destruction which this behavior has brought to other men's lives he assumes will bypass him. Men are not destroyed, as a rule, because a mighty crisis shatters them into the dust. They are destroyed by a number of small habits which, when added all together, spell inefficiency, tawdriness, weakness, and blundering. And every good fellow assures himself that each little evil thing in itself should not be taken too seriously, and no killjoy should be allowed to speak his blunt word concerning it.

Wasting time is one of our great sins, and it has its way with us because we are sure that this particular time will not matter. Why should we drive ourselves to work all the time? Why should we not indulge in our desire for loafing, visiting, and postponing? Why not, indeed? But the pleasant person who is certainly well liked finds out that minutes turn into hours and hours turn into days. He discovers that life is short and opportunities do not linger very long. He discovers that he has been ruined by an easygoing hopefulness which life denied.

One of my closest friends is a physician, and he told me one time that it was hard to consider men as sane creatures when he saw what terrible chances they took with their health. Things that mean death will be trifled with in the name of relaxation; strains are imposed on the human body which are criminal, but they are done in the name of conviviality. By hoping that the blundering wrong will right itself somehow, men sometimes live the last years of their lives as invalids or go to early graves because the necessary saving discipline would not be practiced. A shallow optimism is indeed an evil thing.

An unwillingness to come to terms with the unpleasant makes the ultimate disaster inevitable, for there comes a time when it is too late to put off reaping what has been sown. A minister called on an elderly woman at her request because she was terribly upset. She was a wealthy woman, but for several years past she had been cheating the Bureau of Internal Revenue. Her

113

money was so important to her that she had covered up some of her transactions deliberately and left them unreported on her income-tax return. This worried her terribly, and she was in constant fear that an examiner would discover her evasion and the law would demand her punishment. She confessed to the minister that she could not possibly get through the days if it were not for the literature which a certain "peace of mind"sect sent to her. When she would get most upset, she would read some of this material; and it would comfort her spirit and she could sleep. It never seemed to occur to her, until the minister pointed it out, that she should make restitution, pay her honest debt, and then live at peace with herself, her neighbors, and God. She had always managed to find a sufficient opiate from the literature to make her believe that everything would turn out all right and she could keep her money. I think she is more typical of our time than we have realized, and we go our way toward an inevitable accounting because we will not face ourselves and our ethics honestly.

We have our share of politicians whose philosophy is to keep facts from the public for as long as possible. The political leader who truly serves the people is one who is not afraid to let them know the facts, for a democracy is based upon the proposition that the people must know. The mark of the demagogue is his assumption that he knows what is best, and if an economic, political, or moral danger does not get into the public press, it can be dealt with at a later time and he can enjoy prestige and power in the meantime. When in the midst of one of England's most dangerous hours a leader dared to declare how bad things were and what sacrifices had to be made, the British people entered into one of their finest hours. To let a nation think that all is well when all is not well is betrayal.

Preachers fall into this same trap and win a certain popularity and gain a certain following because they always insist there is good news to-night. They heal the people lightly and bring special comfort to those who are already comfortable. In their desire to do so much for so few, such men have betrayed their commissions and no longer speak for the living God. The words Paul addressed to Timothy are still good words for every preacher to hear: "For the time is coming when people will not endure sound teaching, but having itching ears they will accumulate for themselves teachers to suit their own likings, and will turn away from listening to the truth and wander into myths. As for you, always be steady, endure suffering, do the work of an evangelist, fulfill your ministry." (II Tim. 4:3-5.)

It is the biblical implication that a preacher has to do more than give the people just what they want. His is the task of penetrating the shallow optimism of the generation in order to bring men face to face with reality.

Halford Luccock reminds us that in the *Life of Henry Irving,* written by Irving's grandson, there is recounted an item of nineteenth-century theatrical history. Dramatic performances were to be presented only in certain theaters which had been granted a monopoly, but there was no such limit on operas or plays with music. So in some places where licenses could not be obtained, someone gave one loud bang on the piano at the beginning of the play; and that made it an opera. There are those who believe that one good shout of optimism changes a situation and makes it hopeful. But you can no more change the way things are by a shout than you can produce an opera with one bang on the piano. In a day when men seem to think that all is well, a man who speaks for God has to explode the false optimism and reveal the evil that it seeks to cover.

116

2. Despair a Sin

Said Lloyd George, "No army can march on a retreating mind." Men cannot live on the basis of despair, and society cannot endure without hope. The one thing the pessimists overlook, when they seek to make of their pessimism a workable philosophy, is the ultimate nature of man. It is not a matter of whether one likes it or not, but simply that men cannot live in the atmosphere of constant anxiety. This is another way of saying that they cannot live without God, even when they proclaim that they are atheists. Human life was made for hope even as lungs were made for air. To put it in another way, the ultimate battle is always the struggle between faith and doubt; and the only victory which really counts is the victory of faith.

Despair is a sin, because despair is not realistic. Samuel Johnson said one time in a dour mood that second marriage is the triumph of hope over experience. But this is not true, because every man knows many examples of second marriages which turned out happily and successfully. You can argue it the other way just as well and say that second marriage is a testimony to the bliss of a previous marriage experience. If you are to be realistic about life, you

117

must take into account the sudden flash of sunshine out of a dark sky, the unexpected and undeserved goodness which is done by an ordinary man whom you least expected to act that way. Just when we think we are safe and can dismiss some situation or some person as being hopelessly evil, a wonderful act is performed which destroys the whole theory. One of the most distressing things the pessimist has to face is the time when his pessimism is betrayed by men, and he is forced to account for a decency which according to his theory was never there. Which is to say that if uncritical optimism is an evil, so is uncritical despair.

One of the encouraging things a man can do is look back on the dire prophecies which have been made in days not too long past. Remember those experts who told us what the outcome of the Second World War would be—how long it would take to win a victory? I can remember yet hearing it "proved" that Germany could never be conquered because the closer you came to her homeland, the more impossible advance would be. I heard military experts describe how long it would take to conquer Japan, because of the islands which she occupied. Step by step across the Pacific our invasion armies would have to go, and in each case tremendous sacrifices of life would be demanded before we could win back these islands of the Pacific. And none of this could be compared with the cost of invading the homeland of Japan. But all this was wrong, for the islands were bypassed, and a new bomb made invasion unnecessary.

We have been immersed in all the dark prophecies concerning the future success of the Russians. We have been led to believe that everything must go wrong with us and everything must go right with them. We apparently have problems, but they have none. We have every disadvantage, but they have every advantage. It would seem sometimes that the struggle is in vain because in some strange way we have to face economic facts, but they do not; and while we will have to spend money, there is a different answer for them. I think it is time to realize that we have great resources and great allies, and if democracy is all that we claim it to be, we have tremendous propaganda power. It would be foolish to assume that the struggle is about over and that we shall win automatically. But it is just as foolish to assume that our enemy is free from the hard economic, political, and geographical facts which confront all nations.

The future of the world is always of serious concern to all of us, and we would like to believe

that the world in which our children are to live
will be a better one than we have known. The
usual prophecy is that such will not be the case
and that indeed there may be no world at all for
the next generation. That may be true, but I
doubt it. There have been too many previous
prophecies which failed to take into account
some of the unseen elements and some of the
unknown qualities. The bad news which makes
the headlines colors our thinking and defines our
attitudes. We need a still, small voice telling us of
the good news of hopeful happenings in our
world. The future may be a very ominous one,
but there are things about it which cannot but
lift up our hearts.

If we stop to consider the possibilities which
are now in our hands, it becomes apparent that
we are a generation blessed with more potential
greatness than any generation that has thus far
appeared on the earth. The unlimited sources of
power which have come to us mean that men can
be set free from most of the slave toil which
has condemned millions of their brothers to live
only half lives. The despairing prophecies help to
bring about the things which they decry. The
gloominess which denies faith becomes a factor in
causing the black future which it describes. The
assumption that God is not, and that evil can

120

never be curbed, is a blasphemy which is uttered by too many men in difficult times.

That sensitive, troubled spirit of the eighteenth century William Cowper wrote these lines in one of his hymns:

> Ye fearful saints, fresh courage take;
> The clouds ye so much dread
> Are big with mercy, and shall break
> In blessings on your head.

The man who looks back upon his life has to confess that sometimes the clouds which filled his sky were big with mercy. He did not see it at the time, and he may have rebelled against the loss of his sun, but the future proved that instead of yielding to black despair he should have waited patiently to see if God proposed to shower blessings upon him. The generation that desires to be realistic had better face up to the oft-proved fact of human experience, that despair is not realism.

Despair of course is atheism. It assumes that there is no King of the universe, no power making for righteousness. It believes only what it sees and has no proper comprehension of the spiritual forces of the world. Dante could describe hell as a place where hope had to be abandoned. He understood that when God is not present,

121

hope goes too. But if a man believes in God and has a sense of his presence, he can never give way to despair.

We do not realize it, but whenever we say the situation is hopeless, we are speaking blasphemy. Who said it is hopeless, and who are we that we can determine what the Almighty's plans may be? How do we know but that the Holy Spirit is even now moving into the hearts of cruel men? How can we be so sure that God is not going to use this wrath to praise him? Is any man wise enough to comprehend all the height and breadth and depth of a situation so that he can proclaim its limits with assurance? The man who speaks for God does not blaspheme in this manner, but he waits patiently, and he endures with the faith to believe that the last word will be spoken not by men but by God.

It is blasphemy when one speaks of another man as hopeless. No matter how he may appear to us, God's miracle of grace can work for him as it has worked so often for us. One reason Jesus disturbed his contemporaries was his unwillingness to look down on certain groups in society. Strange how men could get things so completely twisted and how they could say he blasphemed because he saw possibilities in men and dared to offer them the power and forgiveness of God. It is too easy to divide society into neat little sections and place the unlovely ones beyond our concern. It will not do, and a hundred times more evil than the profanity one hears on the street is the cold, hard, hopeless word which one may speak against his brother.

Let us not forget finally that it is blasphemous to say that we are hopeless. What man among us has not come to a terrible moment when he lost confidence in himself? It was no longer a matter of blaming the situation or blaming one's neighbors. Now at last he had to face up to the seeming hopelessness of further struggle for mastery and power. The alcoholic is the prime example, when he arrives at the point of no return; and he knows that left to himself he is lost. But that is the moment when God moves in to make clear that with him all things are possible. There are times when the greatest miracle of all is my salvation from despair concerning myself.

It has become a habit for us to think that abject pessimism is a sign of bravery and courage. We sometimes assume unconsciously that this point of view is to be admired because at least it is honest. It is nothing of the kind. It is false; it is sinful; it is full of human pride, and it is a

123

denial of God. If the man who speaks for God will not speak a futile optimism, neither will he speak a hopeless despair.

Our generation has become so aware of the limitations of human nature that it has lost a proper perspective of the power of faith. Standing face to face with all the obstacles, it cannot quite imagine the divine power which overcomes them. The words of the late Sir Arthur Stanley Eddington of Cambridge speak to our condition:

I am standing on the threshold about to enter a room. It is a complicated business. In the first place I must shove against an atmosphere pressing with a force of fourteen pounds on every square inch of my body. I must make sure of landing on a plank travelling at twenty miles a second around the sun. I must do this while hanging from a round planet, head outward into space, and with a wind of ether blowing at no one knows how many miles a second through every interstice of my body. The plank has no solidity of substance. To step on it is like stepping on a swarm of flies. Shall I not slip through? Verily it is easier for a camel to pass through the eye of a needle than for a scientific man to pass through a door. And whether this door be a barn door or a church door, it would be wiser that he should consent to be an ordinary man and walk in rather than wait until all the difficulties involved in a scientific ingress are resolved.[1]

[1] *The Nature of the Physical World.* Used by permission of Cambridge University Press.

The prayer we need to repeat is the one uttered by the father of the sick child whom the disciples could not heal. "I believe; help my unbelief!" (Mark 9:24.) This is a Christian prayer, for it recognizes the underlying faith by which men live, and it has searched the reality of God and his power. At the same time it knows how prone we are to believe things in general and deny them specifically. It is the cry which comes from a soul knowing that there is an answer, but afraid to believe that God can speak just now out of the silence. He who speaks for God brings men the courage of faith as they face the limitations of their doubt.

There are some contemporary signs of a return to religion, it is true. But for the most part the return is neither wholehearted nor profound. It is an attempt to bring the comfort of religion to individual spirits torn with anguish and filled with emptiness. The return to religion, if it is really legitimate, is a return to the hope that comes when men's confidence in God's ultimate victory has been restored. It is not comfort that we need so much as faith, which will put our despair in its proper perspective and show us the glorious things that God has in mind for his children. To be saved from despair is not only to be comforted in our own life, but to see God in

125

history, in personal relations, and to be aware of him as the Lord of the future. Despair does not march, nor sing, nor conquer; it seeks only a holding action and a containment. He who speaks for God sounds the trumpets of hope.

3. Hope a Christian Virtue

We have not paid enough attention to the New Testament insistence that hope is the mark of a Christian. No matter what the outward circumstances may be or what the immediate future may hold, it was the assumption of the men who were close to Jesus that they would always be confident and joyful. Paul goes so far as to say that we are saved by hope, and perhaps this element of our salvation is more basic than we have realized. Certainly it is true that Paul's despair was a mark of the Law's failure to answer his human needs. His entrance into the Christian experience brought him salvation, which in turn overthrew the despair and enthroned hope in his life from that time forward. The New Testament assumes that if a man falls into a period of bleak despondency and hopelessness, it must mean that he has drifted away from God. The men who walked with Christ were always men big with hope.

One of the main emphases which John Wesley

brought back into Christian preaching was the neglected note of confidence. His opponents criticized him because of an enthusiasm which seemed to them far out of bounds. They were not willing to agree that a man might know his sins were forgiven nor that the ignorant and brutal could find salvation. One of the most startling things about the preaching of John Wesley in the eighteenth century was its wonderful promise in the name of Jesus. Methodism became a singing fellowship, and it never leaned far in the direction of depravity. Even in our time Methodism has been defined by a national magazine as the typical American church, because of its optimism.

It may be that Methodists have carried this too far, although John Wesley was certainly aware of sin and its power. He felt then, and perhaps it is particularly true today also, that the world needed an affirmative word. The theological despondency which has been so characteristic of the continent of Europe has spread everywhere and has had a deep affect upon American theological thinking. We have been overdue, no doubt, for an experience of greater depth which would counteract the characteristic shallowness of too much American Christianity. But let us not forget that the good news of the gospel is funda-

127

mentally the good news of hope. And let us not be ashamed to proclaim clearly and emphatically that the Christian faith is an antidote for despair.

We are hopeful because we are heavenbound. This has an unpleasant note to many a present-day critic, because he is certain that a religion that even mentions heaven is a religion that has become altogether otherworldly. Not so! We will be the first to grant that religion can fall into the trap of being irrelevant for today by concerning itself too exclusively with life after death. But once we begin to despise this eternal nature of ours, then everything goes wrong with us here and now. It would be a good thing if every Sunday morning in every church of the land we would sing an Easter hymn to remind us that Jesus Christ has risen and we are destined for eternity and fellowship with him.

Once men take their eyes off heaven, the things of earth seem to lose their sweetness and go sour. Strange it is that when men seek to live nobly in terms of this world alone, their nobleness withers and this planet becomes a prison house. To live worthily now, men must have the long look and the heavenly vision. They must come to terms with the fact that they are on an eternal pilgrimage which colors even tomorrow's labor.

128

This sense of the eternal life is like a secret warmth a man carries around with him in the coldest environment, and it throws a constant illumination on his path in the midst of darkness. We should not say, "All this, and heaven too," but rather, "Heaven, and all this too." The decisive element is heaven and not earth.

The words of one of our greatest contemporary theologians are to the point here:

Nothing that is worth doing can be achieved in our lifetime; therefore we must be saved by hope. Nothing which is true or beautiful or good makes complete sense in any immediate context of history; therefore we must be saved by faith. Nothing we do, however virtuous, can be accomplished alone; therefore we are saved by love. No virtuous act is quite as virtuous from the standpoint of our friend or foe as it is from our standpoint. Therefore we must be saved by the final form of love which is forgiveness.[2]

A woman was teaching a class of working girls in London's East End, and she asked them what the word "bore" meant. None of them knew the meaning of that word, although one thought it must refer to being lost in deep thought. But as Bernard Berenson remarked concerning the incident, this happened about fifty years ago; and

[2] Reinhold Niebuhr, *The Irony of American History* (New York: Chas. Scribner's Sons, 1952), p. 63.

by now "uplift" may have taught such girls what it means to be bored.[3] All the amazing cleverness which has produced so many gadgets for our comfort and ease still has not succeeded in turning this world into a satisfactory place in itself for men to dwell. It is disturbing to note how often boredom has accompanied progress, and hopelessness has appeared when the other world has faded from the minds of men.

But the Christian hope is founded also in the Christian fellowship. Halford Luccock comments on the fellowship which is to be observed among people who have to get up early in the morning. The waitress, as she serves the coffee to the early worker, exhibits a kinder camaraderie than she shows to the ordinary diner later in the day. In the early days of my ministry I began going down to my office at 6:00 A.M. I met another fellow nearly every morning at the corner of the church, and finally we began to talk together for a few moments. I found he was a young lawyer who had the ambition to be the best lawyer in the state of California. I wanted to be the best preacher in the nation, and we were both going to our offices early to prepare ourselves to become the best members of our pro-

[3] *Rumor and Reflection* (New York: Simon & Schuster, Inc., 1952), p. 214.

fession possible. There grew up between us a friendship which meant a great deal to me, and it was founded on the early-morning meetings. The true fellowship always grows out of the relationship of people who are united in a common task and who are working together for a common goal.

There is a sense in which work is the real meaning of the Church and the real secret of its fellowship. It is not just a matter of sitting in the congregation with others, but it is being bound together in a common enterprise which is nothing less than preparing the way for God's coming into human life and society. When with one mind we come together to worship and dedicate ourselves to service, we become a part of something that holds us steady, strengthens us, and puts a singing into our hearts.

How much this Christian fellowship has meant to me through the years! There are times when things go wrong and when evil tendencies in society seem to win the applause of too many people. Good things are shoved aside and trampled. There are days like these, when second-rate politicians go to the top and keep in the headlines by spreading scandal based on rumor and hit-and-run tactics. But there comes to my mind in these times all those brethren of mine across the nation who fight this denial of our Christian heritage and who will never yield to the pressure of the demagogue. I think of the ministers around the world I have met who are fighting their battles in their own places with devotion and courage. Because we belong together, I can never believe that evil can overthrow the fellowship which we represent. I think of the laymen of the churches whose loyalty to freedom and human dignity never wavers and who keep the Church strong and inviolable in the face of the attacks of its enemies. I am not alone, and the fellowship gives me a hope which the world, the flesh, and the devil can never destroy.

During the war a general went out to see for himself the condition of the outposts. He came to a ridge and dropped down beside a soldier straining his eyes into the darkness ahead, keeping the enemy under observation. Telling the soldier who he was, he asked for the boy's name; then he spread out a map, and with a shaded flashlight he pointed out where the enemy was deployed and where his own forces were stationed. Then he took a pin from his uniform and brought it down on the map. "There you are, Private Blank," said the general, "and if you and all the others do their duty, we've got the enemy whacked to the wide."[4] So there comes to the Christian Army the Commander in Chief, who stops beside us and tells us about the big campaign. Then he points out in a new way just where we are and what our job is. He gives us his promise that if we do our duty, the victory will be ours. Hearts that were heavy become light again, and spirits which have been full of darkness are illuminated; the creeping despair which smothered our courage flees away, and hope fills our minds. For we have heaven and the Christian fellowship and the Lord Jesus Christ.

4. Hope from God

Well has Zechariah defined men as God's "prisoners of hope." But it is a kind of prison experience that is real freedom, and we learn finally that there is no other source of hope than God.

W. T. Stace of Princeton is not an orthodox Christian by any means, but if he is not a man of faith, he is certainly not a man given over entirely to doubt. If he does not accept the affirmations of religion, he can see through the

[4] J. T. Davies, *Lord of All* (New York and Nashville: Abingdon Press, 1951), p. 110.

133

false pretensions of its enemies. He writes with convincing logic when he points out the absurd assumptions of some of the popular, materialistic attacks on Christianity. In one book he says that an agnostic in England wrote to him at the time of his country's greatest crisis in modern times. France had fallen, and Britain was fighting alone, with many a person in the United States believing that its downfall was only a question of time. Yet this man wrote with confidence that the British would win the war even if the United States did not enter it. When Stace inquired as to how he could believe such a thing, the man answered that "it is impossible for a system based on lies, such as Hitler's, to prevail." [5] Here was a faith that denied the logic of the man's agnosticism. He found it was impossible to believe in Hitler's ultimate victory, because he assumed subconsciously that the world is a moral order upheld by a moral power. If such men would follow their vague confidence to its ultimate source, they would discover God. The fact that men are saved by hope and that they cannot live without it seems to me a very clear sign pointing directly to God. The further men move away from God's presence, the nearer they move to-

[5] *Religion and the Modern Mind* (Philadelphia: J. B. Lippincott Co., 1952), p. 48.

ward despair. At last we learn that he has made us for himself, and without him there is no basis for hope.

Men have tried many times to base their confidence on other foundations than God. They have tried to build it on humanism and scientism. There are a few stubborn souls who still maintain that this is possible, but the great bulk of mankind knows now that human nature itself furnishes no basis for confidence and the worship of science does not guarantee salvation. Amazingly enough this has penetrated into the consciousness of scientists themselves, and the moral homilies coming from their laboratories are rather encouraging if they are not coming too late. Part of the despair of our time springs from the disillusionment of watching great hopes go down into the quicksand of our secular failures.

There seems to be an increasing appreciation of the fact that psychiatry based on the wrong foundation cannot go nearly as far as it needs to go to bring healing to broken minds and spirits. With our typical confidence in scientific procedure we assumed for a time that we could deal with mental processes on a purely rational basis without the spiritual element of faith entering into our consideration. We do not despise what

has been accomplished in the field by psychia-
trists who have revealed many a hidden secret
about the way men think. But there seems to be a
growing understanding that men are not healed
until they find moral purpose, and personalities
remain twisted until faith and love are recovered.
There is a growing consciousness that psychiatry
can be no substitute for God.

If you have ever tried to explain the game of
baseball to a man who knew nothing about it, you
realize how much of the game lies in the realm
of values and assumptions which are not easily
put into words. You cannot talk about anything
of any significance at all unless you already know
the basis of the truth upon which it rests. This
has been the mistake of our generation in dealing with man and his problems. Having failed to
understand the basis of the truth of man, we
skate on the surface and come up with some
ingenious theories, most of which are only half
true at best and lead us down side paths instead
of on the straight road. It is wonderful to behold
how Christ brought hope to the pagan world because he ministered to man's spiritual nature
and needs.

A member of the House of Commons who had
listened to the wartime speeches of Neville
Chamberlain and Winston Churchill made this

comment: "When Mr. Chamberlain said the fine, true thing, it was like a faint air played on a pipe and lost on the wind at once. When Mr. Churchill said it, it was like an organ filling the church, and we all went out refreshed and resolute to do or die." [6] And this is the difference between the promises of men and the promises of God. Human promises are like thin pipings which fade away quickly. When God gives us a promise, it comes with the fullness of the organ in the cathedral, filling us with courage and determination. Resting on his promises, men through the years have been made strong again. All the others are well-meaning enough when they try to encourage us, but it is only the man speaking for God who can bring us hope. Our confidence is not to be in our seeming strength or our military superiority. Our confidence is to be in the Almighty, whose plans include not only us but all mankind.

There came back from the war a number of young men whose faces had been shot away. In spite of all the skill of a plastic surgeon they remained horrible to behold. When a young wife came and looked at her mutilated husband for the

[6] Sir Alan Patrick Herbert, *The Independent Member* (New York: Doubleday & Co., Inc., 1950), p. 120.

first time, too often she went out unable to stand it and applied for a divorce. One could not really blame such a girl, for she remembered her young husband going off to the war healthy and whole. How could she be expected to tie her life to such deformity and spend all the years ahead in the presence of such horror? But there were a few who managed to adjust themselves and establish a new life with their husbands. The doctor in charge of the hospital came to these young women and told them if they would be counselors and friends to every young woman who had to face what they had faced, perhaps the suicides and divorces could be lessened. They agreed, and whenever a girl had to go through that horrible experience, they came to her and said, "Now look here, we know what you are going through, for we have gone through it. But we know also it can be done. It gets better, and love can still make your marriage a joy. We will be your friends, and we will stay by you just as long as you need us." This was the only thing that worked.

So in these times when it seems that we cannot go on, it is God in Christ who comes to us and tells us that he has been through all this and more, and that he will hold us steady and see us through the difficulty. The hope he brings us springs not out of any promise of escape but out of endurance and spiritual victory. We can look at the worst and believe in the best. This is the greatest word any man has to speak to his brethren. He who speaks for God speaks for a hope that is unconquerable and everlasting.